Chasing the
Dance of Life

—a faith journey—

Cynthia Winton-Henry

the apocryphile press
BERKELEY, CA
www.apocryphile.org

apocryphile press
BERKELEY, CA

Apocryphile Press
1700 Shattuck Ave #81
Berkeley, CA 94709
www.apocryphile.org

ISBN: 1-933993-69-3

Contents

Dedication

To my teachers:
Judith Rock who taught that words dance,
Barbara Elliott, feminist guide
Doug Adams who rallied a generation of artist-theologians
and the Muse who makes myth out of known and unknown,

Spin the tale, let these stories fly.
For I know this:
Story and song are soul speech
but when we dance we make fire.

Introduction

"We have made no progress towards explaining how the
mind is attached to the body."
—SIR HERBERT LOUIS, 1ST VISCOUNT SAMUEL 1870-1963

SITTING ON A PLANE, IT'S HARD TO TELL the guy next to me
what I do. Even after decades of attempts at answering his question,
it still stops me in my tracks. I could say I study theology, art, and
multicultural education, that I'm a community organizer, dance pro-
ducer, former seminary teacher, or a cofounder of a non-profit. I
rarely mention that I am an ex-minister as this can lead to long conversations. I know what I do, but how do I explain it? If I say that I
chase the dance of life and foster freedom what will my seatmate
say?

"You foster freedom? How do you do that?" the plane guy wants
to know.

"Through a non-profit organization called Body Wisdom that pro-
motes InterPlay in fifty cities."

"InterPlay? What's that?"

As the airplane leaves the ground, memories zip across my mind.
My companion does not know that I've sought to answer his ques-
tion all my adult years. I flash back to dancing with Phil Porter and
Judith Rock in Body and Soul Dance Company in 1979. We stum-

bled onto something that modern religion, science, business, and education overlooks. Concealed in the abandoned territory of play, amidst the simplest elements of singing, moving, and telling stories we uncovered a gold mine of body wisdom, the stuff of enlightenment, ecstatic community, and right relationship. People we taught could find peace and health doing things as easy and childish as playing follow the leader. Our discovery led Phil and me to a café table in 1989. With the zeal that usually goes into getting elected for political office or researching a cure for cancer, together we cooked up a crazy scheme to have fun and change the world.

I know better than to burden my seatmate with my struggle to articulate a theo-kinetic philosophy. He doesn't want to hear about the challenge to eke out the easiest route for skeptical, shy, wary, heady folk to regain access to their body wisdom. Worse, if I tell my unsuspecting listener that InterPlay replaced my need for institutional religion, it could confirm me as a flaky, new age kook. Instead, I flip through a menu of elevator speeches and say something like, "InterPlay is a toolset that reduces stress and builds cultures of peace," or "InterPlay is a system of ideas and practices that helps people thrive as they change." Or, "InterPlay helps people play again. Once that happens, anything is possible." If I speak with authority my seatmate might say, "Cool!" and change the subject. I always forget to mention *What the Body Wants*, the book I wrote with thirty of my closest InterPlay friends.

As the plane levels off at an altitude of 30,000 feet, an absurd elevation that no one ever wants to contemplate, I touch the bracelet given to me after 9/11 with the dangling ring inscribed with one word. "Freedom." Frankly, I spend too much time trying to explain what I do. All I know is that thanks to InterPlay, I am getting a paycheck to operate on eight cylinders in a two-cylinder world.

How did InterPlay happen? Ask Phil. He'll tell you a funny, wonderful, sane story. My version is wilder. Perhaps because from an early age I was caught in the tailwind of the cosmic dance, the Great Mystery that no one can describe but that anyone can ride.

If you find yourself inexplicably swept off your feet as I have been, I offer my story as companionship. Along with hundreds, even thousands of mystics, poets, visionaries, and dancers I offer my own chase and the insane, insatiable quest to know why something as expansive, rejuvenating, visionary, heart opening, and socially healing as the dance of life could be so hard to claim.

Fortunately, there are voices that say, "Fear not." On discouraging days I cling to incantations like that of poet Muriel Rukeyser.

> *Let poems and bodies love and be given to air,*
> *Earth having us real in her seasons, our fire and savor;*
> *And reader, love well, imagine forward, for*
> *All of the testaments are in your favor.*

1 | *Fire in My Flesh*

Your very flesh shall be a great poem and have the richest fluency not only in its words but in the silent lines of its lips and face and between the lashes of your eyes and in every motion and joint of your body."
—WALT WHITMAN

OK, I ADMIT IT. I HEAR VOICES. I SEE THINGS. Especially when I dance. Flannery O'Connor said, "You shall know the truth and the truth shall make you odd." I've had mystical experiences that are barely footnoted in America's everyday lexicon and charted my life course by them. As a result my work is not only difficult to describe, I can't decide what to wear to work—a suit, a funny hat, a robe, or sweatpants? Being the Gemini I am, I change costumes as needed.

What do you do if you hear voices or see things? As an American woman with plenty of common sense, I'll tell you what you should do. You should shut up. However, if there are voices that prod you to quench the thirst for big human needs like Love, Justice, and Freedom, you might become a blabbermouth performance artist like me. You might try to demystify dance, healing rituals, and communal peacemaking enough to wave a flag in sight of the mainstream. The Voice of Love is that compelling. Mechtilde de Magdeberg, a twelfth century mystic said, "Love transforms, love makes empty hearts overflow. This happens even more when we have to struggle through without assurance all unready for the play of love." She understood.

By the time I was thirty I was well prepared for the voice that gave me my "instructions." Driving down the freeway on my way to see a horrific movie about nuclear holocaust, a neutral voice simply and clearly spoke to me and said, "Here are your three directives: Clarity of Vision. Efficiency of Energy. Courage to Love." Being both undeniably gullible and unflinchingly faithful, I listened, not realizing I was downloading a mystic's grocery list.

The voices I hear are always wiser than I am. Their messages are to the point, astute, and take me off guard. When I share them with other people they often ask me to repeat them. Should I warn them that when you actually follow the advice you get from "on high" you get into trouble? Things that make sense in a spiritual realm can make you look unusual in ordinary time. "Voices" have incited me to dance in academia, sing improvisational ditties at United Nations Association meetings, and confess mystical encounters from rational, left-leaning pulpits. They made me an iconoclastic prophet of the body and its one true love, play. In spite of all of my best attempts at being taken seriously, my voices have doomed me.

Today, I live on the bread of dance and sense things on freeways and in malls that others do or don't see—spirits, voices, hungers, and curses. Hunting for a tribal dance to feed the soul, I gather people to song, story, beat, and breath. I seduce the cosmic dance out of a thousand starry gaps. I ponder all of this constantly like a mad scientist. Add my troublesome tendency to wax poetic and use jargon that people don't quite get, and you get my problem. Chasing the dance of life inspires me like nothing else. It has also gotten me into trouble.

You'd think that dancing and loving the Divine would create bliss, but putting these two together is like playing with dynamite. Maybe that's why the western world split them apart. Anytime you put your body where your spirit is even the mundane becomes extraordinary.

Jeremiah, that insanely upset Old Testament prophet scribed, "I will not mention God, I will not speak in God's name any more. But then it becomes a fire burning in my heart, imprisoned in my bones; I grow weary holding it in, and I cannot." Jeremiah's pals called him a laughingstock. No one wants to go that far over the edge of mystery, be denounced for loving God, or cursed as touchy feely. Not Jeremiah. Not me. But the costs of shutting down the wild ambushes of compassionate imagination are also great. I've met many a person whose body screamed with the symptoms of repressed dreams. Their throats are on fire and their bowels scream with ulcers. Giving up one's imagination isn't worth the price of admission you pay to a "dominant" culture.

I've reassured myself that the ancestors knew what they were doing. They sent us into the woods to receive visions and meet our guides. Initiations and vision quests gave us strength to do great work. Thank God I am an artist. When I tire of trying to fit in I remember that an artist who isn't weird is in the wrong profession.

So why go on about this? Because I believe that it is our weird lives that lead to answers needed for a world in dire shape. I think we need to reclaim our wisest magic, not the puff and zap kind, but the kind that employs imagination to attract solutions when nothing else works. In my case, dancing, improvising, seeing things, and listening to the wisdom of my body has shown me how to accelerate peace and grace in a world that dances too vigorously, too mechanically, and too violently. I've seen peace born between people who bring their hand to a partner's hand in an extemporaneous, experimental two-minute hand dance. I've seen walls crumble as a person describes to a coworker what they had for breakfast, a favorite place in their home, or someone who has come to their mind. Without effort people can move mountains of division. I've even seen individuals recover from depression to take on their life's work with the support of an imaginative, embodied community.

The big challenge is creating a society that is willing to bet its future on such practices. Usually it's only the desperate who are open to radically simple and crazy ideas: the poor, the sick, the imprisoned, women, the disabled, the oppressed, visionaries in developing countries, people of color, the usual revolutionary suspects.

I learned that you have to be sneaky to subvert the average person's self-conscious fear of flakiness. If you want to nudge someone to fall down the rabbit hole of mysticism into Wonderland, humor helps. So do parables and enticing, insignificant little steps.

Once in a worship service with an academic crowd, I placed boxes of corn flakes on pedestals. We confessed our overwhelming fear of flakiness and how fear keeps us from admitting our strangest encounters with each other and the Divine. From puberty, it too often keeps us from doing normal things like dancing, laughing, breathing, and offering affection. I should know. My own fear of flakiness is why I wrote all this down. There is some relief in seeing one's truth in black and white.

G. K. Chesterton said, "There is a road from the eye to the heart that does not go through the intellect." Where does it go? In my case, the roads of perception go straight through my body. But, as the daughter of well-intentioned Protestant Christians, I'm rational by default. My dad was a Methodist. Method is a word I appreciate. But dullness is a drag. The church of my youth tended toward emotionally blasé. Leaders droned through Bible stories about insane people who heard voices, followed stars, and beheld visions that changed history as if they were trying to make relationship with an unseen God sound like a Hallmark card. WASPiness was anti-spice. Anything provocative was typically doctored in neutral shades of tolerance if mentioned at all. Faithfulness was defined by sitting in pews, wearing clothes you never rolled around in, showing off fifth grade reading skills, feeling bad for the needy, and never acting like the crazy people in the Bible. Resurrection of the body, the weirdest, coolest idea of all, was a doctrine that no one would get near.

We kids knew that dulling down the spirit wasn't natural even to Methodists. It was just for show. Trying to sound and act calm was a pretend way to have the peace of Christ.

Fortunately, the ministers knew the Word of God was best found beyond words. Reverend Ray Ragsdale hired a Hollywood choreographer for our high school youth choir presentation of *Joseph and the Amazing Technicolor Dreamcoat*. Youth camps that linked nature, God, firelight and song awakened my most basic spiritual instincts and in college, Mike Fink, the campus minister reinforced that song, dance, and telling ancient stories were medicine for the soul.

Consequently, I fell in love with the faith of my father. But I itched for something more. I didn't want to be a Holy Roller. I only knew that faith needed more than reason, control, and seriousness. I already had plenty of that as a girl zealously afraid of displeasing anyone.

I was devout by the time I was fifteen which is why it came as a surprise to discover that I was also religiously unruly. My soul was allergic to taking things too seriously. At my first communion I knelt with a dozen white-frocked youth. As the minister stuck a wafer on my tongue, I broke into uncontrollable giggles. I couldn't contain myself. The story of my life. Maybe it was because they made me a member of the Body of Christ without real credentials. Or, maybe it was because amusement flows directly from joy and joy is my birthright. Or maybe it was the kneeling. Kneeling always gets me in trouble. A church lady gave the youth group free Bibles under the condition that we get on our knees to pray, and I thought, "Ha! Show me a kid that prays on their knees." It was 1970. But her Bible was free, so I got down on boney kneecaps with the rest of them.

Or, maybe I caught the giggles out of an instinctual reaction to religion's serious face. My path needed to be crooked and swirl like a labyrinth. The first time I saw a labyrinth chalked on a floor in a wisdom university my reaction was to skip. Joy is like that. But, spontaneous joy and skipping are hard to find in Protestant Land. Actually, they are hard to find in any part of American adulthood, even the arts.

I think my gut instincts were good. If I took things too seriously, I'd ruin everything. I am prone to being a driven, addictively right-eous, scared out of my mind, meaning-monger. To dance this life, I have to let go of it. If I hold onto steps, attitudes, beliefs, institutions, or meanings, nothing works. Dancing saves me. Not the steps or choreography, but the irrepressible energy that rushes through when

I trust the universe to move me. The fabulous poets in the Hebrew Bible confirm this. Proverbs says,

> *When God established the heavens*
> *I was there*
> *When God drew a circle on the face of the deep*
> *When God made firm the skies above...*
> *Then I was beside God*
> *Like a little child, a playmate,*
> *Rejoicing before God always*
> *Rejoicing in God's inhabited world*
> *And delighting in the people of God.*

Like many an eldest child, I am a born caretaker. But, the dance of life sprouted up like a magic bean in my psychic backyard, anyway, making even my birthplace, Kokomo, Indiana, sound mirthful. In some ways it was. My grand folks dreamed of easy street. Grandma fed us giant bowls of ice cream for dinner. In spite of the small town Methodism, none of my relatives were opposed to dance. So, when the family gathered around the radio and Elvis Presley crooned, "He Ain't Nothin' But a Hound Dog," I bounced up and down and got my first applause.

I inherited excellent kinesthetic genes. Mom was a competitive roller skater who pulled off ballet duets on eight wheels. Dad was a lifelong athlete in everything from judo and ping-pong to hundred-mile mountain races. The two of them met in the skating rink. Unfortunately, fun had a way of turning sour in my family. The family tree was riddled with alcoholism, gambling, and zealous disciples who found either God or their drug of choice. When things got hard, which they often did, my people had a habit of joining other opportunity seekers and laborers who picked up and moved. Mom's family specialized in doing people's dirty laundry. Dad's people farmed, worked as electricians and janitors.

Thanks to the GI Bill and the Korean War, my father was the first

Winton in generations to go to college. Graduating from Purdue University as an engineer, he landed a job in Santa Monica, California, where I got my first dance lessons at Miss Vivian's store-front studio. Miss Vivian was an MGM film-cutter with dreams of stardom. Under her direction I debuted in the cavernous Veteran's Auditorium. I lined up with dozens of tutued tykes and I missed my cue. I was horrified but it didn't seem to matter to Miss Vivian or Grandma. Miss Vivian gave me a ballet dancer music box. Grandma took me to lunch at the International House of Pancakes, praised me as only a grandma can and admitted me into that rare club of dancers who don't remember cues or steps but still feel like stars.

The dance of life wanted me. Like a zillion other young girls, I fell in love with ballet. When Mom and Dad took me to see Swan Lake, I perched on the edge of my red velvet seat. The lights went out. Music swelled and the curtain slashed open. Glorious, fragile, dreamy swans danced, using a heart-language I knew was mine. Through strains of Tchaikovsky's *Swan Lake* the dancers summoned me saying, "Cindy, you are a dancer." It was my first clue that you could dance your dreams. To this day, if I hear Swan Lake on the radio or in an elevator, my body aches like a tuning fork, and remembers.

My imagination grew kinesthetic wings and allowed me to sense invisible things as if they were really there. When a kindergarten teacher told the class to line up, I lifted the edges of my pink dress and pretended I was being escorted to my throne. The teacher noticed and said, "Look at what a good job Cindy is doing." Imagination got me extra credit.

Making up stuff worked great in the daylight but in the dark, there were recurring dreams that terrified me. In one I stood with mom on the bow of a ship on the lake of snakes. Dad and a gang of sailors held the legs of a giant spider and slowly, menacingly approached us. Peering overboard I was afraid I'd fall in.

There was also that gnarly, ugly burnt blob that repeatedly appeared in my day dreams, only to be transformed into a white, glowing ball. I was seventeen when I learned the secret of this apparition, a secret I am not allowed to tell.

꙳

Dad's engineering job catapulted us from a Santa Monica bungalow into a ranch style tract home with a driveway on which I jumped rope, practiced fake ballet, and pretended to be Little Joe from the TV show Bonanza. I couldn't play on the dicondra lawn, but building forts out of cut grass in the field behind the house was fine. I found freedom in wild places.

Each evening I set the table for dinner and rhythmically recited

Salt and pepper
Sugar, butter
Milk and water
Bread and jelly
And sometimes Kool-Aid.

All was well, except when it wasn't. Spankings from dad were to be avoided. I could avoid them if I told on myself. Truth had a strange effect on my parents. They quieted down. Like the time I hung from the bathroom towel rack, ripped it out of the wall, reported the misdeed and was forgiven. Yet, I never told a soul about the day that I unscrewed the red stick handle off of my brother's push toy, walked to the corner of my cul-de-sac and did what traffic control people do. I stuck out my red stick with panache and waved a passing car onto my street. As she turned into the cul-de-sac, the driver glared, embarrassed to be under the spell of an eight-year-old. I dropped the stick and ran home, certain of being arrested for impersonating an authority.

꙳

At my ballet school a girl with pink toe shoes stretched her leg straight up the wall. My leg didn't do that. Kids called me Skinny

Bones Jones. I had turn-in, not turnout. Plus the teacher ignored me. Even though I loved dressing up as "spring" in my blue tutu with pink roses, when Mom asked me to choose between ballet and Girl Scouts, I stashed the tutu in my hope chest. I didn't need ballet that bad. Besides, I could make my little brother, Danny watch me improvise the entire *Swan Lake* record.

When my sister, Valerie was born, the house shrank. The family moved to a tract home in Harbor City, walking distance from the low-income projects. Our elementary school had kids from every background. My sixth grade teacher, Mr. Laney, looked like Dr. Martin Luther King, Jr. and rewarded me for all the things I loved to do: write, dress up, dance, and cooperate. At graduation he asked me to convey the class theme "I Have a Dream" in a dance. That's when I performed my first hand dance wearing a white homemade dress and fire-red fake fingernails purchased from Kmart. I was glad to illustrate the lyrics from *South Pacific.*

> *Happy talky talky, happy talk*
> *Talk about things you'd like to do.*
> *If you don't have a dream,*
> *And I don't have a dream,*
> *How you gonna have a dream come true?*

I grew up at a time when a kid in Junior High could take a modern dance class instead of go to regular gym. The teacher, Mrs. Tuttle, a bird-shaped woman, loved to swing and swoop. It felt like cheating, it was so much fun. The first time I tried choreography, unexpected ideas exploded in my brain. I gasped and stuffed my hand over my mouth to hold in the explosions. Thinking with my entire being was ecstatic. But, who gasps in the middle of gym?

Every year Mrs. Tuttle gave me A's. Unfortunately, kinesthetic aptitude was never tested on California State Achievement tests. I had no hint that I might have a gift until the school winter assembly. Costuming four girls in white leotards and tree tinsel, I shaped lunges, leaps, and synchronized legwork to "I'm Dreaming of A White Christmas." The next day in front of English class, the teacher praised me. Deep down, I smiled.

✿

After ninth grade ended I went to a backpacking camp with a bag of jeans, T-shirts, the book given to us by Methodist camp leaders called *No More Plastic Jesus*, and a heart full of questions like, "Will boys look at me?" Hiking to the High Sierra base camp was a cinch. I'd followed Dad dozens of times over mountain trails and could compete with the fastest boys. But, at night the girl who played the ukulele with her swishy long hair, easy laugh, and firelight beauty made me jealous. I had pimples and greasy bangs.

During free time I dug out *No More Plastic Jesus*. In the blue-lit tube tent I read that God doesn't care about money or looks, just people. I looked out at the trees, heard the junior high laughter and wondered what it meant.

The week climaxed with the supreme social test: communion. We climbed up the mountain to a place enclosed by boulders. At sundown each youth was invited to come forward and take communion as the leader said, "Come take a piece of bread." When my turn came, instead of feeling warmly welcomed, intense knots of shyness swelled up in me. I froze and conspicuously proved that I didn't belong. Another night came and went and I was still unpopular.

Hiking out the next day misery should have hounded me. Instead, a miracle happened. One book closed and another opened. Out of nowhere I looked at the sky and sensed that God loved me equal to everything else. I had no memory of making a conscious shift. I was simply breathing, smiling, and open. And for the first time, even boys talked to me. What a miracle!

At the car, Mom knew something had happened. She asked what was different, but I couldn't say. Maybe puberty slipped out the back door and took its spastic hormones with it or maybe Jesus' unplastic poetry coded itself on my heart in my sleep. Whatever happened, I felt like dancing. The Jim Strathdee camp song made sense. Grace was more than a dance word. It was in me.

> *I am the light of the world*
> *You people come and follow me*
> *If you follow and love*
> *You'll learn the mystery*
> *Of what you were meant to do and be.*

The feeling lasted a week until my little brother, Danny, irritated me so much I screamed and blamed him for breaking the spell. It wasn't easy being a junior mystic.

Shortly afterwards Danny had a stroke. The house grew tense. Dad's anger erupted. Although he tried to make up for it with flowers and hugs, Mom imploded between one hospital and the next. Her fingers typed out a Morse code of furious letters on the steering wheel of the car as we waited at stoplights.

Neither vacations, new furniture, nor church repaired what broke. Without counselors or guides to help us withstand the turmoil that pounded us, our formal living room turned into a theater of threatening conversations that began with sentences like, "Honey, Grandma was killed in a car accident." And, "Your mom and I are separating."

I stopped dancing in the living room, clung to security, and bawled the day the Goodwill truck drove away with the ugly, green, high-backed chair that had held me each night as I watched T.V.

⚜

How does a teenage mystic find a guide—broadcast molecular messages: "Dancing Spirit Seeks Tribe," "Sensitive Teen Seeks Help to Unleash Healing Powers," "Daughter Seeks People Who Dance to Pray"? In the seventies with no web to Google, no chat rooms, blogs, or links to point me to teachers, the dance of life had to find me on its own, and it did.

Mrs. Mac taught public high school modern dance. Her female

students felt better after warming up to songs like "Love is Blue." But, dance led me to more than better feelings. Movement activated unknown worlds. Mrs. Mac saw this and gave me leadership of the hundred-member drill team. I learned to design formations and yell across football fields. During halftimes we marched onto the field in green miniskirts and black bolero hats as the Gauchos. We performed intricate collective routines in stark contrast to the grunting game of the boys. But, just like the boys, I used the whole force of my body to lead.

At the kitchen counter I asked Mom, "How do you get to be popular?"

Having had almost no experience of this she gave me her best guess, "Smile?"

With that advice I left the house each morning, rolled up both my skirt and the corners of my mouth. Everything was up, up, up. I was either a teenaged Alice in Wonderland or the Cheshire cat. By junior year Mom's suggestion worked. Scooter Townsend, my first true love, asked me to the Homecoming Dance.

I was sixteen when Reverend Ray Ragsdale asked me to choreograph a dance for Christmas Eve. I'd never seen a religious dance, but it made perfect sense. Anytime I danced I felt closer to God. My best friend, Janice helped me choreograph to "We Three Kings." Although there were only two of us everyone loved it. It was the first time I robed for church—bath-robed.

Next Janice and I choreographed the Lord's Prayer, wearing leotards and tights. When Reverend Ragsdale previewed the dance and watched us lean on the communion table, our legs extended in arabesque, he cleared his throat and said, "Cindy, it won't work to have crotches show that way." He initiated me into the power of sexuality right there in church. I was shocked. Unbidden shame triggered my anger. How could a worshipping body be a problem in God's house? I had no idea, but the look in Reverend Ragsdale's eyes told me to change the dance.

Mrs. Mac also mysteriously knew that I danced in church. She cut across secular-sacred boundaries and placed Doug Adams' book, *Congregational Dancing in Christian Worship* in my hand. Mrs. Mac was a Methodist. On top of that she got my parents' permission to take me to San Diego to meet Reverend Michael Taxer, a former New York City dancer turned Presbyterian minister. We got seats for his dance-drama production, *King David*, performed in his church hall. Mrs. Mac also arranged for me to meet him to talk about dance and ministry. I was seventeen.

By senior year I had long, blond hair and was senior class vice president, drill team president, and a prom princess. Ideas continued popping outrageously in my head. Smiling made it easier to enjoy people. But when my boyfriend, Scooter, voted "Mr. Most Likely to Succeed," succeeded with someone else, revenge was what I wanted. I auditioned for the school musical *Guys and Dolls*, wiped the smile from my face, and sang "What Do You Get When You Fall in Love?" The choreographer cast me as a Latin temptress and hot-box dancer. Scooter took me to the senior prom and when he dropped me off, dumped me. Popular Schmopular.

The end of high school question loomed. "What are you majoring in at college?" I turned to my teacher. "Mrs. Mac, should I major in English, Art, or P.E.?"

"What about dance?" she said.

"You can major in dance?" I exclaimed. This was like being told I could eat all the chocolate I wanted. That's when I put it together: Swan Lake, fire red fingernails, Christmas tinsel flying, "We Three Kings," dancing ideas exploding, the rush of sensing a shape, a meaning. A navigational bell rang, "Do what you love." Supported by my parent's encouragement to follow what I love, along with the voice whispering in my ear, I knew what to do. Follow and love, and learn the mystery of what you were meant to do and be.

That fall, the UCLA dance studio was crammed with fifty new dance majors and the smell of stale sweat. Meeting the faculty was intimidating. They initiated us with these words, "Dance is work. You don't get paid and you hardly get noticed. You only dance for one reason. Because you have to. You must love it. Most of you will be gone before the four years are up. So, if you don't want to do the work, you might as well go now."

I looked around. No one moved. I believed everyone in that room loved to dance. Perhaps we loved it more than when we walked through the door. I did.

The faculty wasn't threatening us, they were alerting us to an awful truth. Dancers have no future in a capitalistic world. Dancers are reminders of transitory life, messengers of a spirited world.

I began my study of technique, learning how not to stick out my butt, how to move from center, how to simultaneously relax and gain control. I learned to work with gravity, fall down and recover, and extend my energy far beyond my limbs. I learned to use my head for more than linear thinking. I could use it as a prop, a weight, a light, a window, and a locus of meaning.

I played with other dancers, encouraged them, and laughed at myself. I was at home. Modern dance had plenty of room for people who had "original" movement styles. Some days as the musician pounded out lyrical strains on the piano, I almost flew.

Like a novice monk, I barely noticed that I was learning universal lessons, lessons that shamans and healers have learned through the ages. Certainly no one pointed out that dance was the medium through which history's spiritual leaders entered trance, took visionary journeys, listened to wisdom and shared dreams. I had no idea that I tinkered with the means for engaging and warding off unseen forces, ways of transferring the wisdom of my body as medicine to another person, shape shifting through space and time while keeping my feet on the ground. None of this was in the syllabus. It was a secret professors don't discuss.

To make a big impression I called my first dance "War and Peace." I quickly learned that three minutes, three dancers and an audiotape of orchestral music don't replicate an epic. To my credit, my vision was already apocalyptic even if my talent wasn't. After I broke a foot in technique class, I choreographed a solo on crutches to elevator music from "Butch Cassidy and the Sundance Kid." The crutch is an amazing prop. I swung and bounced off the walls. The professor said that my choice of music trivialized an otherwise inventive dance. To be honest I didn't care. I was just playing. But, in school, even dancers have to be serious. Maybe more so if it's their only hope of becoming legitimate.

Before long, criticism did its work. My ideas stopped popping. I made spiritless dances about things I didn't care about. In 1975 no one danced about anything personal. The dance formula was "dance for dance's sake." Prayers, Faith, God were never mentioned.

My training and inner life were in conflict. I would never admit that I attended a campus ministry group led by a man called Reverend Mike Fink. Working behind the check out desk of the law library, I was hesitant to mention my major. Dance seemed so inconsequential.

Meanwhile hanging out in the dance department, I watched Martha Graham walk down the hall; I sat at the feet of dance historian Lincoln Kirsten, and looked up from sewing in the costume shop to see Gene Kelly standing in the door. Greatness haunted that place, a greatness that called for greatness.

In the desert a Benedictine monastery annually hosted a week of dance and prayer. Driving onto the property past a sign that said, "No Hunting Except for Peace," I found men in brown robes that sang their prayers five times a day, and more importantly, I found Carla DeSola. Carla directed Omega Dance Company out of New York City's Cathedral of St. John the Divine and had devoted her life to moving in the Spirit. I saw something of myself in her.

Outside of the university I could focus on my inner dance. At school I trained my body and mind. I taught my face to relax, have expressions, and strengthened my technique. Well into my third year, I attempted a ballet combination across the floor and screwed it up. My eyes snagged on my image in the mirror. I started over and screwed up again. A high, gray wall of over-thinking appeared. I had sucked in my gut and studied myself in the mirror too many times. I was in the puberty of technique. The desperation of the feeling required immediate action. That very day I told the head of the department, "I have to stop. I'm not quitting. I'll be back."

I moved to Janice's Long Beach apartment, got a job leading tours on the Queen Mary, found a boyfriend, developed music, dance, and drama liturgies for churches, hung out with a Lutheran student community, and avoided technique class. When September arrived I pulled on a leotard and socks with toes and heels cut out, and walked back onto the UCLA dance studio floor. I danced better than ever.

Peering into the future, I imagined trying my luck in New York City with Carla DeSola's company. But, I also wanted to be helpful. Is dancing helpful? The more I pondered this question, the murkier my vision became. I was overcome by fits of gloom. Anytime I went to church or sang a hymn I'd weep. I knew nothing of despair that mothers extraordinary moments, or of mystics like Saint John of the Cross who scribed, "In the lucky dark, no light to guide, except for my heart this fire inside." If I had known that saints and mystics are friends of depression, despair, and confusion, I might have weathered the storms of restless change with more grace.

Finally some spirit pushed me to ask my dance history professor about dance in church. I knew that once I admitted an interest in religion, there was no going back. Just as I feared, she raised her eyebrows. My credibility quota was in jeopardy. In spite of the look on her face she suggested that I read the autobiography of Ruth St. Denis.

In the early 1900s, after seeing a coffee shop cigarette poster of the Egyptian Goddess Isis, Ruth St. Denis had a vision of the divine dance that took her on a journey around the world to perform dances called "Radha" and "Incense." She began to teach, taught Martha Graham and fell in love with a former Methodist seminarian turned dancer, Ted Shawn. Together they formed Denishawn, one of the birthplaces of American modern dance.

I sat at my kitchen table reading her story. On page 336 I stopped. Her words lit my heart like a torch.

> *I was lying on the couch that was always placed in my dressing room and, with hands clasped behind my head, was in that half wakeful, half-sleeping state which is so often the perfect condition for creative thought. For some moments, feeling the silence of the theater, I remained in a quivering expectancy. Suddenly, looming like a great pearl—like a new Taj Mahal—against the dark shadows of my mind, was a temple. I realized at once this temple was the symbol and the focusing point of my whole dancing life...this cathedral of the future wherein all the arts, as well as the dance, would be summoned from the ends of the earth to become instruments of spiritual beauty.*

Was this my destiny too? Then, I heard a voice say, "Go into the living room." I rose and entered the dim, barely used room with its musty overstuffed sofa and wood floor. The voice said, "Kneel." Even though I still resented the church lady who made us kneel to get a Bible, I knelt without hesitation. As if it longed to happen, energy and light poured into the top of my head and vibrated my spine. I swayed. Was this an invitation to dance? Afraid to break the spell, I stayed still. A window opened in my head. My eyes both grew and disappeared. Then, I apprehended everything in the universe. The feeling that accompanied this sight was pure, neutral, unconditional regard. Nothing unloved. Everything beheld in the same way.

My response was instantaneous. Offering myself to the walls, the air, whatever this was, I would do anything to serve it. Then the feeling lifted. Still on my knees in the same musty room, I got up. Stunned by the holy intercourse, I felt as certifiably weird as a biblical ancestor. Questions ricocheted. Was this a visit from Ruth St. Denis? What did it mean?

I went to my bedroom and wrote about St. Denis' vision of the church of the divine dance and the all-encompassing neutral love. They seemed to be related. That is when I knew. I would dedicate myself to the dance of life and to holding dance and religion together.

Charismatic Christians describe this experience as an anointing. My tradition had no name for it and preferred not to hear about it. The apostle Paul might have had a direct hit from the In-Your-Face God, but reasonable people don't. I wisely suspected that my experience might not make me popular in the Dance Department either. Perhaps this life-changing event happened because only something like it could get me to persistently carry such a call into a world furiously suspicious of the body and still extremely tight-lipped about spirituality.

Was I chasing the dance or did it chase me? Ten seconds emblazoned God's eye on my heart. I called Mike Fink, the campus minister, and told him everything that had happened. The gangly gray-haired man listened to the encounter with Ruth St. Denis, the Church of the Divine Dance, and kneeling in the living room. As if he rehearsed for this moment, Mike pulled a book off his shelf. "Take a look at this," he said as he handed me *The Art of the Rhythmic Choir* by Margaret Fisk. Margaret was a sixty-year-old woman who led dance in a Methodist church in Fresno, California. She had uncovered fragments of the story of dance in Christianity.

Dance in Christianity? Someone else had been entrusted with the dancing soul of a people. Was I part of a hidden lineage, a lineage that went back to Miriam, known as a prophetess because of her ability to sing and dance? I wanted to run out in the street and yell, "See! See! I knew it. I knew it!" But Mike wasn't finished. He handed me a brochure for "A Day on Dance and Religion" led by Doug Adams and Judith Rock at Pacific School of Religion in Berkeley and gave me the plane fare to get there.

Pacific School of Religion, part of a consortium of theological schools called the Graduate Theological Union, sits alongside the University of California in Berkeley. On the quad looking over the San Francisco Bay and the Golden Gate Bridge, I could see why they called this place Holy Hill. The natural beauty took my breath. But, there was something here even holier than that. People danced in the dining hall and library doing medieval dances of death, dances from the early church, and dances with rainbow umbrellas underneath the cross. I learned that Christmas Carols were originally danced, and that carol means, "to dance." The leaders were people for whom dance and faith united. Doug Adams and Judith Rock expressed an intellect that was not divorced from emotion or intuition. They studied theology and art.

I'd found the next step on my path. Angels could not have done a better job of pointing me in the right direction than Rev. Ragsdale, Mrs. Mac, or Mike Fink, the Methodist friends of a dancing God.

Back at UCLA the world looked different. Seeing a sign for the UCLA Art Museum exhibit, "African Art in Motion" I was pulled in. Drums, song, and raffia skirts rushed at me from video screens, instead of artifacts; I saw a living culture where dance occurred everywhere. Gods danced. People danced. Masks, music, sky, and dirt danced. Everything danced together. I heard the echoes of an ancient home, a place where dance guided people through the mysteries that no one can articulate.

A few days later a poster on a cafeteria wall jumped out at me. "Operation Crossroads Africa: Spend summer in an African village." I tucked it in my dance bag, applied, and was accepted. While friends plotted trips to Europe, I raised two thousand dollars from churches, won a President's fellowship grant, and took most of my spring courses in the African Studies department.

The dance professor's prediction was accurate. I was a senior and looking around the department, only a handful of the original fifty students remained. I was one of them. With the senior concert only a month away, I went into my usual choreographic mode. I hid in the studio and when anyone peeked in, self-consciousness guillotined my creative process. In spite of anxiety, I tapped the wellspring found in the desert with Carla de Sola. Inspired by her use of David Karasek's poem, "Images of the Spirit," I blended word, live music, and dance to create "Earth Prayer," my first and only university dance connecting dance with faith.

On the dark stage, I took my place, balanced on one leg. Ignited by Karasek's words I began.

A wind of windless silence roars
A wind
of windless silence
roars,
in the form of stillness
moves,
in the movement of stillness
is.
Moving and forming
stillness dances
a sacred dance upon a thread
a sacred
dance
upon a thread.
In the balance of awe,
the unfolding;
peace.
In the balance
of wonder
the spirit
broods.

In the airborne place of the dance,
in the secret place of the heart,
timelessness created the moment
and the unseen depth
is seen in the flight of grace,
is seen in the flight
of grace.

Through the waterfall
passes the light of
the unseen face
the secret shape,
through
the waterfall.
Falling water.
fall immersing,
fall embracing
the secret shape
the secret shape,
the unseen face,
the secret shape.

Holy flaming
Holy flaming
Holy flaming
leaps in precious tongues
within a womb.
What burning
prancing within a womb aflame!
Laughing humus,
earth prayer,
O joyous flamboyant earth prayer!
Earth,
prayer;
desert bush
O desert bush,
what fire enkindles and loves

> *enkindles and nurtures you?*
> *O joyous flamboyant earth prayer,*
> *O joyous*
> *flamboyant*
> *earth*
> *prayer!*
> *From a dance within a womb*
> *I am born of God the Hilarious Light*
> *O Hilarious Light*
> *O Hilarious Light*
> *Hilarious Light*
> *I am born of God the Hilarious Light!*

On the last words, in a coil I sprung from a squat into the blacked out air. The audience applauded through several bows. I'd finally made something true. Was everyone waiting for me to do it? A professor asked me to audition for her dance company. I tried out and even though I couldn't get all the steps, they asked if I could join them that summer. My trip to Africa won out.

In Sierra Leone, West Africa, eight African-Americans, three white students, and four Sierra Leonians shoved body and bag into a lorry and headed for the village of Tiama. Our assignment was to help build a cultural history museum. While the UCLA Art Museum elevated dance and drum, boom boxes were the prize of every mud thatched home in Sierra Leone.

Everything was unfamiliar: the smells, the tumultuous rain beating on the tin roofs, the creole dialect, the chief's son's hand slipping invasively over my breast in the middle of the day, and the bribery used to get anything done.

We slept at Tiama Elementary School on wire bunks with straw mattresses. Mosquito nets separated us from the bugs that were as long as the Mississippi River. There was so much humidity that the washed clothes never dried.

The museum project was more dream than action. The cement we needed was stuck on ships in the harbor. The only day we worked at shoveling dirt and carrying bricks from one spot to another was to impress the American ambassador as he drove by in his white limo. Fantasies of helping Africa blew away like chaff.

I expected cultural disorientation but was unprepared for the loneliness. Although we were artists, musicians, writers, drummers, and dancers, when I sat down to eat a meal the African-Americans sat elsewhere. Trying to get close, I offered to wash a woman's hair. As I soaped her scalp, she joked with the others about how fun it had been to scare white kids who were bussed in to play football at her high school. I had no clue that she was including me in the intimacy of that moment. I only knew I had been on a bus like that. I felt the excruciating gap between the others and myself. Romantic illusions of dancing with friends evaporated.

"Be a good sport!" I admonished myself.

An inner voice screamed back, "THIS IS NOT GIRL SCOUTS!"

I escaped into J.R.R. Tolkein's *Lord of the Rings*. Hobbits felt more like family.

In spite of this, the dancing spirits found us during the coming out ceremony for village girls. By mid-summer everyone in the village wore a garment made from the same cloth. By word of mouth, we got news that the girls were coming out of the bush. We went to the edge of a clearing. A clump of older women hid the young women under fabric as they moved from the jungle to the chief's house. It was a Bundu ceremony. Drums and shegores beat in rhythm as a dark-masked Bundu Spirit bounded into the circle in front of the chief's house and teased the crowd. The raffia-covered dancer exuberantly tested, blessed, and chased away evil spirits from the people. As one of the secret society of dancers, the Bundu Spirit embodied the most direct contact people had with ancestral guidance. The dancer was God

Everyone joined the dancing. I was in a snaking line of teachers, chiefs, mothers, university workers, lorry drivers, and Americans. Young children tagged on at the end. Simple steps rocked us as we moved in rhythm, winding through this West African village. An older woman broke out in ecstasy. Her naked breasts flew, feeding us with her energy.

At dusk, reggae music replaced traditional rhythms. Hips velcroed together, sexuality steamed. In dance that was more sexual than I'd ever experienced in public or private, God, sex, and power blurred together. The night was fertile and alive. I lost track of time and whether I ate or drank as loneliness evaporated.

The following Sunday morning at Tiama Methodist Church worship, the feeling was discouragingly familiar. People had adopted patterns of individualistic, vertical stiffness. Western reverence shrouded the congregation. There was no dance.

By summer's end I finished Tolkein's trilogy as I navigated constipation, malaria, and vertigo. After a thousand-mile lorry ride to Ghana to board the plane home, "glad to go" was an understatement. Yet, I had uneasy feelings as soon as I reentered the U.S. Peering through L.A.'s automated haze I saw the mechanized west devour life and turn it into trash. The dance of life was buried somewhere under heaps of technology and work. The only means of transport was by automobile and phone. No one seemed to remember that dance is how spirit travels. U.S. girls stop going to dance lessons when they start college. Men and elders dismiss movement as something they don't do and wonder why young people seek altered states and hate office chairs and pews. Tradition no longer moves from body to body. I knew that faith weakens when the young can't feel it in their muscles. Losing the corporate dance, we lost its fruits: communal power, authenticity, cooperation, reconciliation, passion, harmony, and joy. Only the common dance and song can carry corporate body wisdom from generation to generation, mend rifts in social relationships, lift clouds of despair, and move people to common action.

What I saw worried me. My task was more daunting than I'd imagined. How could I support the dance of life? I remembered Pacific School of Religion and sent in an application. Even though I wrote about my strange call they accepted me for the fall of 1978.

Years later in a prophetic exchange with South African church leaders I asked, "When Apartheid ended, I saw Bishop Tutu on the front page of the newspaper dancing. Didn't dance help you get through the difficult days of apartheid?"

"Yes," one of them smiled. "We are a dancing nation."

I said, "In the United States we don't know how to dance joy and sorrow anymore."

He must have sensed my grief because he looked me in the eye and offered the assurance of Lazarus, the man who died and came back to life. He said, "It will come."

Moving back to Long Beach I got a room in an inner city Victorian with Lutheran friends, finished my degree in dance, wrestled with another bout of malaria, and eventually landed a job as an activity director in a convalescent home. Steve Henry applied to rent the room in the attic. A balding Clark Kent, he was a twenty-eight-year-old seminary graduate employed as an alcoholism counselor in a nearby hospital. I said hello, touched his elbow, and warmth flooded my brain.

At a wedding Stephen asked me to dance. Stepping into his arms, I immediately took the lead. "Who's leading?" I asked embarrassed. It's a question we still ask decades later.

I began sneaking up to his attic hideaway, climbing a ladder tucked in the closet of a sleeping housemate. After months of this he finally said the magic words, "I love you" and we rented a dinky one-bedroom apartment on the beach. No more closets. I postponed seminary to spend more time with Stephen. Having grown up in a Baptist church, handing his fate over to God a hundred times, completing clinical pastoral education in an alcoholism unit and enrolling in a PhD program in preaching, he understood the call to seminary. So, in January of 1978 Stephen drove me north to Berkeley and we kissed goodbye.

Doesn't everyone's theological education begin with the apocalypse? The first week at Pacific School of Religion I was cast in professor Wayne Rood's ambitious multimedia production, *OmegAlpha: The Book of Revelation*. I played the white horse of the apocalypse, one of seven deadly sins, and the whore, Babylon. Sex, sin and seminary. I was off to a great start.

Having no money to pay for anything but tuition, I ate in the refectory on weekdays and stole my roommate's peanut butter on weekends. But it was more than just vitamin B-12 deficiency that made my head spin in New and Old Testament classes. Researching Babylon, I noticed how many times Biblical writers personified woman as evil: Eve, Gomer, even Jerusalem were sluts. In rehearsal I danced Babylon's death atop a huge model of the world wearing a white leotard, red cape, and bejeweled mask. The abandoned Methodist cathedral was fittingly gloomy.

Carol Wickersham played the fourth deadly sin, sloth, and pulled me aside one night. A student trustee on full scholarship, she was also an artist who "saw things." When she asked under her breath, "Did you see the huge angel in the back of the church tonight?" I knew she wasn't joking. We bonded for life.

God, sex, and power were not mere metaphorical dilemmas. Costumed in a gold wire horse head and white leotard, I asked Wayne Rood if I needed a bra. I was so flat chested I didn't own one. At UCLA, breasts were no issue, perhaps because dancers were either women or a gay men. When Wayne Rood looked me over in costume he shrugged, unimpressed. But, on opening night Stephen was seriously rattled. When he found words he sputtered, "Why are you showing your nipples to the world?"

"Nipples?" I dumbly asked, looking down at two benign bumps.

Thus began the nipple controversy, a strange undercurrent in my dancing, religious life. Should I cover up? Was I giving myself to everyone in the audience? Was this why dancers and actors are considered morally questionable? Are we really prostitutes, sexual surrogates, and erotic projection screens? What about dancing the Bible! Wasn't this seminary?

I was naive. I clung to an innocent dream that my body was mine and wasn't bad until it was clear Stephen's fears couldn't be soothed. I bought a double A bra and chose relational peace over feminist ideals. Friends raised their eyebrows as I took a little step back-wards. The feminist lioness of the day, Mary Daly, would have been horrified, but she didn't love Stephen.

My future in the church was forecast. I dug into questions like, "Where is the original innocence, the dance of life, among those who claim resurrection of the body?" I found some companionship among theologians like Dietrich Bonhoeffer who said, "We do not 'have' a body; we do not 'have' a soul; rather we are body and soul. In the beginning we are really our bodies...the one who renounces their body renounces their existence before God." Mine was a wild-ly affirming God who holds all things with equal admiration, nipples and crotches included. But what to do with men overwhelmed by sex?

On a bright green March day on our way to the Muir Woods, I nudged Stephen and asked, "Are we going to get married?"

He answered, "That's what I wanted to ask you."

I left school. Stephen and I choreographed a matrimonial dance beneath a willow tree in the backyard of a couple who had nurtured him when he lost his mom at age twelve. Fifty people gathered on a warm September day: my parents on the verge of their divorce, Stephen's eccentric dad, siblings, and good friends. It was a typical American family wedding, a blessed occasion. We hyphenated our names, declared our commitment, honeymooned in the San Juan Islands, and moved to Berkeley so I could finish seminary.

I called Judith Rock when I heard that she'd formed a dance com-pany in Berkeley. A gifted Presbyterian minister and theologian with an MA in dance, she taught courses on dance and theology and was to be my mentor. Not long after arriving in Berkeley, she invited me to perform in "Covenant," where I met Phil Porter. Phil, Judith and I had no idea that we were beginning the ten-year journey of Body and Soul Dance Company. Cast as the junior member of a holy trinity, I traveled with them around the United States and England. Judith gave language to things my soul knew and taught me to love words like living beings. The three of us determined to reunite parts of life that so often seemed split apart, church and theater, humor and sorrow, emotion and craft, skepticism and assurance, word and dance, mystery and clarity, and body and soul. We were ardent disciples of faith and ambiguity.

Trained dancers were rare on Holy Hill but Doug Adams, Pied Piper of Christianity and the Arts, opened doors for artistic understanding throughout the theological academy. I presumed it had always been that way and took it for granted that I could choreograph dances for my classes in Ethics, Old Testament, and Systematic Theology. My professors welcomed my dances even if they didn't know how to grade them. Professor Herb Otwell looked like a CIA agent in a black suit and skinny tie. After researching the prophet Jeremiah's anguished relationship with God, I poured myself into a three and a half minute solo called "Yoke of Rage," and ended with arms crossed in a knot, one pulling toward earth, the other pulling toward heaven. Herb's eyes glued open. After a few minutes of buttoned down speechlessness he had only three words to say, "You got it." Of course, I wrote a paper, too.

With dance as my theological canvas, I played tug of war with the underbelly of faith. I pulled, poked, gnashed, punched, and made fun of my own beliefs. In "Falling" I grappled with my insistent refusal to feel needy. I threw myself to the floor so many times that it made me sick. In "Rachel Weeping" I thrashed out rage at God's indifference to victims of violence. My solos were often brutal. Only when improvising or making a dance with Phil did I find my lightheartedness.

I had no intention of being a minister. I couldn't imagine dedicating my life to a male hierarchical institution. Add to that my greatest fear, public speaking. Ministers talk a lot. However, I did imag-

ine plotting to teach the church to dance. For that I needed credentials. Judith said the best way to be taken seriously was with a religious union card, a Master of Divinity, ordination, the whole
Reverend thing.

I created a seminary lab called the Graduate Theological Union
Community Dancers, hoping to reconcile my desire to serve a
greater purpose with the powerful ability of dance to build community. It turned out I had a knack for teaching. Doug saw my poten-
tial, encouraged me to go for a PhD, arranged a full scholarship, and
asked me to replace Judith as the adjunct faculty in dance and theology.

A wedge of competition was driven into the heart of Body and
Soul. Judith and I were caught in an unhappy game of musical
chairs. Yet we needed each other. It was either courage or survival
that compelled us to take our struggle to the studio. P.W. Martin
said, "The creative process is not constructive only, but has its
destructive side, the nay no less than the yea, there is the dark and
terrible aspect of God, the volcano as well as the rock; creation
comes from conflict." I needed my Rock!

We made the dance "Wrestling with the Angel." Entering from
opposite wings truth awaited us in the form of a single, collapsible
folding chair pitched stage center at an angle.

> *Two women, unusually twinned*
> *driven by a cello's minor chords*
> *approach a single chair*
> *in knifing paths of light.*
> *Sweat curls the hair on their necks,*
> *Drips down backbones sheathed in white*
> *except for the right arms, exposed.*
> *White is the color of truce.*
> *The dance is rally,*
> *competition, chase.*
> *They climb the coveted chair,*
> *their only goal.*
> *Atop to fight, balance,*
> *fall, collapse into each other's fulcrum.*

At last a breath
too deep for words
suspends all body parts
in the unresolved air.
Blessing and hating each other,
neither knows who's winged.

To be ordained one needs a denomination. Stephen and I both decided we were ready. He left the Baptists and I left the Methodists to unite in the Christian Church (Disciples of Christ). Its very name reflected two movements choosing to unite. The next thing needed was a local church to do the honors. The first time we sat amongst the people of Lafayette Christian Church laughter filled the room. Twenty minutes from Berkeley's steamy "don't-give-up-the-struggle" politicism, we took a deep breath among the rolling hills and oak trees that surrounded the sanctuary. Justice was on the agenda, but the place didn't feel like a battleground. The minister, Stan Smith, and the congregation took us in and welcomed my uncommon desire to seduce the church into the dance of life. A hook unfastened in my soul. They didn't question my call, although some worried about its practicality. Could I make a living at something like this?

On Pentecost Sunday, the day of fiery tongues and capital "S" Spirit, I was ordained. Kneeling for the third time in my life, friends, family, and church members laid hands on my twenty-eight year-old head. Under the pressure of so many good wishes, I suddenly realized ordination was more than a union card! I was marrying my work in front of God and everybody. Even so, as it said on the front of the program, "It loved to happen."

2 | Lessons of a Reluctant Master

God is not cool water to be drunk for refreshment. God is fire. You must not only walk on this fire, you must dance. And when you have learned to dance on this fire it becomes cool water, but until you learn to dance—my Lord, what struggle, what agony."

—NIKOS KAZANZAKIS

UP OFF MY KNEES, A MINISTER in the Christian Church (Disciples of Christ), there was one small dilemma. I didn't have a personal relationship with "you know who." This was not something that my seminary seemed to worry about. Theologies about God, Spirit, and Jesus Christ were common fare, but not personal relationships. I began to worry that someday I would be standing in three feet of warm baptismal water with an eight-year-old looking up at me. Her white gown would balloon out around her in the aqua blue tub. A thick silence would fall upon the people as I asked, "Kid, do you believe in Jesus as your personal Lord and Savior? For that matter, do I?" My body couldn't lie. Everyone would know I was an ordained faker.

I began scurrying around my psychic wardrobe like a person forced to run outside in their underwear. Could one have a relationship with Christ without being a jerk, a monk, or a world-forsaking saint? Surely Christendom wasn't based on having a personal relationship with Christ for nothing. A wise friend told me not to worry.

41

He said "personal Lord and Savior" language was just bumper-sticker theology gone badly.

Back in college a student caught me sleeping on the lawn and woke me up to quiz me on The Four Spiritual Laws, "Is Jesus Christ your personal Lord and Savior?" he asked. When I shrugged defensively, he prayed for me. Nothing happened. I wasn't saved, just irritated.

Being an artist didn't help my Jesus connection. I had a list of Jesus conundrums. First of all, art is about experimentation. Christianity isn't. "What Would Jesus Do?" never seemed like an open-ended question. Number two: Artists rarely painted Jesus' picture in those days unless he was in the shadows. Number three: I struggled with the conservative bent in the Christian world that split the world into Christ-centered vs. world-centered, body vs. spirit, good vs. evil. I couldn't imagine being devoted to a diabolical Christ who insisted that I "be good." I was already too good. What I needed was to get real. The more I thought about the whole Lord and Savior idea the more it bugged me. What about people who couldn't use this magic password?

I wanted to pick up my faith and head for the nearest closet. Sure I measured my decisions and actions by his, but I often forgot who was the Savior. Seminary didn't help. It was the perfect spiritual armoire, hiding anything that didn't dress up in intellectual formulas. Professors rarely discussed personal relationships, especially with Jesus. I suppose everyone was fending off some hard-nosed beast referred to as the Christian Right, but no one would mention it. We didn't want to be judgmental.

How could I answer the only words that my denomination required I commit to? Deducing that it must be possible even for a hesitant feminist like me to say the words "personal relationship with Jesus," I finally started praying for a personal relationship with him (whatever that meant). This was one of those times I could have been more careful about what I prayed for. I awoke from a dream in a sweat, disturbed by a face that appeared before me. A dark-skinned, persecuted Latin American Indian with messy black straw hair looked me hard in the eye and in a deep neutral voice said, "This is the face of Jesus Christ."

His face was irreversibly stamped on the back of my eyelids. I blinked hard thinking, "No wonder I don't want a personal relationship with this guy." What was I to do? Go to Latin America? No. Give my life to the poor? Learn Spanish? I was language disabled. If that was my path, this Jesus found the wrong disciple. But the face of this indigenous Southern Hemisphere man began haunting me.

The very first time I crossed the Richmond Bridge to visit Pacific School of Religion, (PSR), I drove through the oil tanks, ratty industrial port buildings, low-income houses, and depressed, treeless streets and thought, "I never want to live here." Unfortunately, this was before I learned the never rule. Never say never.

Stephen and I got ordained but Stephen got the real job in a small Richmond church less than seven miles from PSR. We rented a bungalow on Rumrill Road, a mile from the dump and downwind of the Chevron Refinery. When we wanted fresh air and scenery we joked, "Let's go to the landfill!" Each evening, semi trucks shifted from first to second gear directly outside our bedroom window. We played New Age music to drown out the grinding gears. On Sundays I played minister's wife. My duties included sitting in the pew behind the woman who often faked having a seizure during worship, going out after church to a local eatery with the seventy-year-old "Out to Lunch Bunch," and occasionally teaching Sunday school. Children were the only ones interested in embodied creativity.

I sometimes wore my hair in a bun and tried to dress conservatively, but costumes didn't disguise my true nature. Everyone knew I danced with Body and Soul, was a consultant for creative worship, and had entered the doctoral program in theology and the arts. Fancy-shmancy, artsy-fartsy. Some church ladies weren't too keen on me. Perhaps because I danced at Stephen's ordination. Or maybe because we released balloons that first Easter. Or maybe it was white-collar blue-collar, military-conscientious objector differences. Then again, maybe it was my breasts. I was paranoid. Truthfully, I didn't fit the minister's wife stereotype. When Stephen and I proposed that the church hire me quarter-time to develop their non-existent education program it was partly because we needed money. His salary was the lowest in the region. At a church board meeting it went to a vote and I was pleased to be hired. But it turned out there was a higher law in the church and I broke it—the law of ministers' wives. It is clearly scribed in the historical codes of memory that a minister's wife is sacrificial, always there when needed and never paid. I didn't realize how much the idea of hiring me would offend the ladies. They got busy and the next Sunday the congregation rescinded the vote, claiming to lack a two-thirds majority.

For three years the church grew in discomfort instead of size. Stephen wasn't immune. Our marriage suffered. Stress chewed on us like an ornery cow. We got therapists.

More and more, Richmond depressed me. Men in giant yellow space suits cleaned toxic waste from a stream a half-mile from our house. The city's cancer rate was the highest in the nation. I felt like I was living on the butt of a bad suburban dream. Buying a green velvet country-style sofa and love seat from J.C. Penney was like taking an environmental antacid.

Why did I choose to live this way? A therapist gave me a personality test and I scored zero out of one hundred points for material need. He raised his eyebrows and suggested I factor in living in the world! "No one is a zero," he said.

I hadn't grown up poor. Maybe it was my grandparents' fault. They were cleaning ladies, telephone operators, laundry workers, and motel managers. One grandfather liked to gamble and lived off of disability after falling from a beam at the Delco Electronic plant in Kokomo. The other Grandfather had a hard time staying sober and often disappeared. The blanket I inherited had been his wool wino house, a cover for a checkered past.

Maybe I tolerated my poverty because I was an artist. Kinky Freidman said, "Every great artist should be ahead of his time and behind in his rent."

When church and home felt like hell, I could easily escape in dance and art. On tour in Great Britain, I got to reach up to the ribbons of light shooting across the high cathedral arches. In Edinburgh I wore a gown the colors of an illuminated manuscript to dance the pregnant Mary in the candlelit Anglican Cathedral. At Coventry Cathedral, on the heated marble floor, I raised my arms in a mirror image of the towering green tapestry of Christ. The stare of onlookers didn't matter as the thundering vibrations of the organ matched my passion. Even as I performed "Pieta" in a California church fellowship hall I knew my wealth. I had a gift that created a freedom found nowhere else, the freedom to possess my body, sexuality, passion, and ecstatic love for God right out in the open.

※

The dance of life begged me to find it. I came upon witnesses who spoke of it like Nietzsche who said, "You must carry chaos within you to give birth to a dancing star," and the scientist, Virginia Stem Owens, who said in *And the Trees Clapped Their Hands: Faith, Perception and the New Physics*, "I carry about in my body, in a single cell, the pattern of the universe. I am pregnant with the cosmos. And in Tasmania, buried in a manioc root, is my body. Select a spot, put your finger down anywhere and you touch the stars. Pay attention to it, and from your fingerprint, like the rays of an aura photograph, reality radiates, meaning sets out, rippling over the immense ocean of energy until it has fabricated the entire universe."

The Bible became a place to listen for the sounds of feet dancing and eyes uplifted. It was all there hidden in ancient languages, old footnotes, and in the spaces between the words. The dance of life ignited my own poetic imagination. As Judith had promised, the words themselves began to dance.

> *What is the space in these laughing cells?*
> *the arcing light in a dance?*
> *What is the buoying elegance of energy?*
> *the song singing itself in each tribe?*
> *What is the tonic of forest, cliff, sea,*
> *the trillion tendrils of sensation in my fingertips,*
> *the noiseless voices that leap to my brain?*
> *What are the arms of love's neutral harbor?*

What is the name of this unanswered joy?
this knowing?
and what story shall we choose to track this cosmic dance?
Christ's name?
The native people's?
the unfathomable monk's?
our own?
Body upon body
spirit upon spirit
eternal, inextricable
tangible bodyspirit
What does the fire want,
and the watery void
and the earth
and the spirit
if not to dance?
To dance is to let go into holy desire.

Reproductive instincts nagged at Stephen and me. When a parishioner found a lost dog in the mountains we went to check it out. Peering through the fence, a purebred Walker hound latched onto us with anxious eyes. It had mange and smelled of desperation. I vigorously shook my head no. Unfortunately, a fatal glance back toward the fence wiped away our intelligence. The next thing I knew the dog was in the car. Maybe it was a gene thing. In a snapshot of Grandpa Winton he was surrounded by a pack of Walker hounds. "Coon dogs," as he called them, were great for catching squirrel back in Indiana.

We named our dog PK, an abbreviation for preacher's kid, and went home by way of the pet store to procure pills, ointment, a collar, and fifty pounds of dog food. PK looked relieved as I filled a bowl with food, set it on our backyard driveway, and sat down to enjoy our new dog's first meal. PK froze, grrrrrrrrrring a low, ominous growl. Then her eyes locked on her tail as if it was a predator.

In a masochistic fit she chased, bit, and drew blood from her tail. Neither Stephen nor I could stop her.

I wept.

Every time we fed PK it was the same. After months of reassuring her, stroking and talking to her, we eventually put her in the garage at mealtimes to protect ourselves from her self-inflicted terrorism. That was not our only challenge. Walker hounds roll in horse dung, live in packs, and run like crazy. Shutting her in the garage or tying her to a tree was the opposite of freedom. We learned our lesson. We weren't right for PK.

We put an ad in the paper. A man answered the ad, and drove up in a pick-up truck fitted with a gun rack. His eight-year-old daughter, named Cindy, knocked on the door. PK met them at the screen. It opened and she ran outside, jumped in the front seat of their truck and never looked back. Stephen and I looked at each other, mouths open. She hadn't even said goodbye.

PK's role was bigger than that of a foster dog. She had become my spiritual teacher. In a class on prayer, professor Flora Wuellner led a meditation to heal our inner wounded child. As the class fell quiet, a hundred faces relaxed. Flora encouraged us not to force ourselves to heal or change. She said, "Force is contrary to God's nature. Go to sleep if you prefer." My eyes closed. Instead of sleeping, a big-breasted opera singer with a spear charged back and forth across the proscenium of my psyche. Zooming into the foreground, she threatened me, "Don't mess around here!"

I assured my boisterous inner protector, "I'll be O.K." and with that she disappeared. In moments a rabid dog appeared. Panic was screwed into her eyes as she violently shook her bloody prey in her mouth.

Flora's voice coached, "Invite the Divine."

At her suggestion another dog appeared, a wolf that kept a distance from the frenzied hound. It was Christ. The wounded dog fixed its crazed eyes on Christ and tore up the mountain. On top of the ridge it howled. The Christ-dog howled nearby.

When Flora called us back from meditation my eyes and face were wet with tears. I sat in my chair considering what had just happened. Who could I tell that Jesus Christ appeared as my personal

Dog and Savior? No one ever mentioned anything about having a personal relationship with a dog.

Stress from church intensified. Marital challenges moved from relational low boil to bubbling trouble. Stephen grew distant. I over-worked myself for little pay. An artistic beggar, I put out my hand for coins and scraps, but never got quite enough to survive on. My calendar was so full I felt poor in time. Stephen accused me of being all over the place. It was true. I didn't belong anywhere. Recognition was almost non-existent. My name was frequently missing or misspelled in programs and church bulletins. At age 29 I was nobody, with no time, and no place. I wanted to bust out of low ceilings of hope, trash blowing across my front yard, and toxic poison in the gullies around me.

With marital hari-kari imminent, Stephen and I headed north to Trinity County. Behind a locked iron gate that read Oddfellows 1942, a dirt road led us to the cabin my Grandpa built. Not fancy or even quaint, it was a rock in my life, a place I'd gone since childhood. Perched above a creek, grandpa constructed it from the remains of torn-apart houses, made a picture window from a meat case glass, and laid a checked linoleum kitchen floor that was worn out when he put it in. The place had more nails than wood since grandpa used his hammer for therapy.

Everyone with a cabin at the camp had to become an Oddfellow, including me. Odd meant you believed in helping orphans, widows, and burying the dead. An odd female was called a Rebecca. My grandmother was one. She was proud when I told her I was to be initiated into the order. I wore a fancy dress for the ritualistic procession that culminated in uttering the secret password, "Love Your Neighbor." It wasn't that different from other odd fellows I hung out with.

Once at the cabin, safe inside the heavenly gate, questions about the future lay between Stephen and me in bed each night. The pitch-black was no comfort. We took walks, watched deer gather at dusk, and remembered the six good years we'd had. The morning of our departure we sat on a wooden bridge and talked about what lay ahead. Marriage? This ministry? Things could go either way.

Stephen and I got our butts into marriage counseling, went on a "thin-within" diet, and bought a new Mazda pickup with everything on it. We felt rich and planned a long vacation away from the church to visit dimly remembered aunts and uncles in the Midwest. In Taylorville, Illinois, Stephen's grandfather once had a successful pastorate. It was there that my thirty-nine year old husband confessed to having chest pains. The local emergency room diagnosed it as stress. The church a thousand miles away loomed like a hungry dinosaur waiting to gobble up our hearts.

I grabbed his hand and proposed, "Let's try co-pastoring! Maybe two people can do the impossible job of one minister." I didn't want to be a minister's wife, but maybe I could be a minister.

Our prayers were answered one month later when we interviewed at a Silicon Valley church full of engineers. They were just like my Dad. We drove to the suburban neighborhood, not unhappy to see chain restaurants and no evidence of toxic waste. I put on hose, pumps, and a suit. Phil, from Body and Soul, shook his head warning, "Artists can't be pastors."

Arriving early for our interview, we took time to pray at a nearby park. Closing my eyes I saw a path appear. It led out across a flat prairie. Without warning, a nuclear blast blossomed in a full mushroom on the horizon. I popped open my eyes to see manicured trees and picnic tables. I tucked the scary image away, not to give it a second thought.

The interview was fantastic. Church members knew of my creative worship talent. We brought bread, wine and flowers and shared communion. In retrospect it was a little like having intercourse on the first date. I only worried when a petite woman happily chirped, "We never have any conflict here." That was the first time I saw the red button that could set off a nuclear device. One week later we were hired.

The highlight of the going away party at the Richmond church was a liturgical dance done by a big, hairy guy dressed in floaty dance attire. I cried and cried. I couldn't stop laughing.

The church Stephen and I inherited had a dismantled organizational structure. The interim minister had done an amazing job of helping people realize that the old ways weren't working. There were no bylaws, no committees, and no consensus. Talk about creativity. The church was in a complete state of spiritual remodel. Members were camped out, cooking over their liturgical camp stoves, and wondering why they couldn't use the old stuff they'd hauled out to the parking lot. They gradually developed spiritually sour breath and came to meetings with furrowed foreheads. Young members were thrilled to be on a spiritual adventure, already convinced that a seventy-five-member congregation didn't need twelve committees. But soon even they wanted to know, "How do we put this mess back together?"

As co-pastors, Stephen and I were as fan-dangled new as all the other changes. Everyone expected us to bring life to the community, but first they wanted someone to clean up the mess. As a thirty-one-year-old female I was bubblier, more direct, and opinionated than my spouse. Even so, church members welcomed me and my claim to fame, creative worship and…drum roll…dance. I set about to change the seating arrangement in worship, adjusting their flexible worship space to create a softer semi circle. Stephen was against it. His last church taught him about the perils of change. But I had authority, and I was going to use it.

※

Stephen and I fantasized about having our own upscale, suburban home like those of parishioners, but all we could afford was the kind of bungalow we'd left in Richmond. The church graciously raised a down payment for a small house with two front yard pines that shed the meanest needles in the world. The view from the living room looked out on a knot of electrical crossed wires, the same view we'd had at the Richmond house.

At the realtors office we had our pictures taken. Smiling in shock, the deed was done. We owed the church.

During our first year in ministry, I was Little Red Riding Hood who set off to deliver pastoral ministry goodies to her grandma. Skipping along I was soon to discover that Grandma had big teeth.

No one in seminary ever said, "Cynthia, don't be creative, be strategic!" I'd been told that the church needed artists. Nor did the seminary mention that women ministers shouldn't change anything in the church. It was only after I was installed that someone commented that just being a female in church leadership was change enough and don't mess with anything for five years. I got a lot of ideas in seminary, but skipped the internship.

My second year as a pastor a thin gray haze gathered. Had we made a mistake? I hated preaching from a pulpit that was stuck to a wall, so I preached from the floor. Maybe that was what started the grass fire. Maybe I reminded people of their aunt or daughter, the crazy one. Maybe it was my legs. At the communion table a male elder whispered to me after praying over the bread and juice, "You have great legs!" Checking to see if I was fully robed, I confirmed that my clergy gown hit the floor and replied, "Thank you?" The guy was harmless. But the comment was bizarre.

Admittedly, the problem could've been the nude body suit. I invited the church to attend a farewell performance of Body and Soul Dance Company. Judith was moving to New York City. I trusted that my parishioners would enjoy the humorous dances like the country western version of Sarah and Abraham's life journey, "Sadie and Abe," or the elegant "Merry Meeting" between those two pregnant mothers, Mary and Elizabeth. Heck, the dances were biblical!

Honestly, it was not until I pulled on my costume for "Snake Charming," a dance about Eve and the snake before "the fall" that it hit me that I was about to go onstage in a nude unitard with one arm featured as the green snake. Church members recently from Iowa were going to see the exact shape of my butt, not to mention my pokey little nipples. Unitarded female ministers playing with apples and snakes? That might have started the mutiny.

Pentecost Sunday is a day Christians celebrate the in-breaking Spirit. I put on my robe and danced down the linoleum aisle waving ribbons of fire. The dance was subdued but joyful as I placed the banner near a small fan. The flames moved gracefully. Unbeknownst to me more than air hit that particular fan.

A month later when Stephen and I returned from vacation the elders said, "Please don't dance in worship."

I couldn't believe it. I could kick myself. I felt abandoned, and misunderstood. Would elders tell a minister who had a degree in history to stop talking about it? Would they tell a minister who performs jazz saxophone, don't play that here? Shattered, I began repeating the unspoken western puritanical church codes to remind myself of what I forgot in that Pentecost moment of devotional stupidity.

> *Thou shalt not have a body,*
> *Nor move thy body.*
> *Nor indicate any life force*
> *Beneath thine robes.*
> *Thou shalt not dance*
> *or cavort.*
> *Thou shall work hard*
> *Walk in straight lines*
> *And hold fast to thy pulpit.*

I got mad. Once again it seemed the male elders were firing Eve, making her the devil. Were they worried I might break into uncontrollable ecstasy? When they asked me to stop dancing, it felt like they asked me to stop being free, open, loving, my ideas popping. It felt like they were asking me to stop being me.

Deb, one of my denomination's first lesbian ministers, knew my plight. She told me the church likes to harness deviants to its back and turn them into burdens. Lesbians and dancing female ministers had things in common. Embodied, empowered women are too much for status-quo religion. Dance was taboo. Sex was taboo. Female bodies were taboo. Sexual inner authority was too, too taboo. Gay and lesbian oppression felt kindred to my own. Homophobia and body phobia are twin symptoms of a common fear. Claiming one's sexuality can scare people.

I didn't know how to move forward. Teach the congregation that they needed dance or hold my course? All I knew was that my primary vision of the church of a dancing God was cut off at the knees. I comforted myself by remembering that artists are pot stirrers and mess makers. Artists don't bring balm to well-housed, well-spoken, well-rooted marchers of tradition. The leaders of my church were disturbed. Looking into the eyes of parishioners, I wanted to love the Lover behind the fear, but it was hard.

In the following weeks, Judith moved away, Body and Soul ended, and I had a job where dance was not welcome.

Spiritual leaders need divine help. People who sit in the pews bring unfathomable wounds and unanswerable questions. Over the top empathy meant that I caught the depression of others before they even admitted they were sad. And an entire church body swelled up with spiritual trauma? Empathy could kill me. I needed help.

Turning to Flora Wuellner I asked, ""Do I really have to pray?"

"Do you have to brush your teeth? If you don't your teeth will fall out. Prayer is like that. Church leaders who don't pray suffer," she answered.

I imagined a toothless preacher gumming her way through a sermon. I didn't enjoy brushing my teeth but luckily, they were still in good shape. Still, the tone of her voice gave me pause. I needed help.

I couldn't imagine praying to some Sunday School Jesus, dark faced El Salvadoran, or even wolf-dog Jesus. I wondered if it was too late to investigate another tradition. But Buddhism had all that sitting. Native Americans complained that white people robbed them of everything, and Goddess worship was problematic since I had only known God as a genderless neutral energy.

An inner voice gently encouraged, "Keep the faith and befriend your history."

Wasn't I sitting in the home of one of the great Protestant prayer teachers of my time? Why not go for it?

Flora and I began to pray for my relationship with Christ. With my eyes closed, I let images and body sensations come and go. It didn't take long for an exuberant man to flash into view. Jesus. He was the quintessential playmate. Even his eyes laughed. Dancing gregariously, we played follow the leader, switching leadership back and forth. I immediately loved this dance, this dancer. Then we faced each other in stillness. Face to face with Jesus, I felt tension knife through me, like the terror of being raped or violated.

I turned away and faced the stars pleading, "God, please, whatever this is, help me." Was this the kind of prayer Flora was talking about?

My personal relationship with Christ was not all peace and joy. I left Flora's house sensing Christ as both playmate and threat. Hating intense spiritual discomfort, I made an emergency appointment with Phyllis Magal, an artist and former PSR student who developed her gift of clairvoyance through the Berkeley Psychic Institute. She was the only one I could think of who could look at my spiritual angst and give me an honest reading.

Her kitchen had no candles, red drapes, or crystal balls; just mugs of coffee, newspaper piled on the table, and dishes in the sink. As soon as we sat down Phyllis smiled. She laughed easily. This always reassured me. She closed her eyes while inviting me to keep mine open.

"Say your whole name," she began.

"Cynthia Lee Winton-Henry."

With both feet on the ground she prayed for God's blessing and asked that her reading benefit us both. Then she said, "O.K., what do you want to look at?"

"It's my relationship with Christ. I seem to be afraid of him."

I watched her face. She looked curious, as though she thoroughly enjoyed looking at the backside of her eyeballs. I knew she saw things. So did I. Even though we were daughters of engineers and doctors, we had confirmed that images held wisdom. Being a seer was like any other gift. It needed tools, practice, and a healthy ethic.

Finally she said, "It looks like you lived in the time of Christ."

I dashed to my inner Bible to find my favorite character, the woman who anointed Jesus' feet with her hair, Mary Magdalene.

But Phyllis didn't see a woman. She asked, "Who was that guy that decided not to follow Jesus? Oh yeah. The rich young ruler. You were a Jewish leader."

Rich young ruler? My least favorite Bible character! I was severely wary of rich people and money phobic.

In the gospels, the rich young ruler asked Jesus, "What do I need to do to inherit eternal life?

Jesus replied, "Go, sell everything you have, give it to the poor, and you will have treasure in heaven; and come, follow me."

But the young man turned away sad. The text says that Jesus was sad as well.

Suddenly, my financial life passed before my eyes. At age six I wrote my first book about a poor girl whose family survived a whole week on twenty-five cents. At age eleven my Mom took me to lunch at Macy's Department Store. Sitting among fancy, white-gloved ladies I wanted to crawl under the table with shame. Why? I had no problem spending money on art and worship. But having chosen the two most underpaid professions in the U.S., dance and ministry, I couldn't pay my bills, lived in depressed neighborhoods, and feared the ultimate doom of being trapped behind a mall department store register as a sales person, a job I knew how to do. All the while, deep down I was a tri-level, four-bedroom-with-a-den suburban-bred woman.

Phyllis' voice broke through my economic nightmare. "It looks like you were a part of the group that set up the crucifixion."

"What?" I blurted, not sure I heard her right. The involuntary pain pierced my chest again. It was one thing to play with images, but another to have truth stab you in your chest. I slid backward down the excruciating silence of two thousand years. It was guilt that knifed my heart. Jesus! It's hard to be with someone you helped to kill.

Phyllis spoke, "You knew it was wrong to kill him and have been trying to make up for it ever since."

I sat in horror as the ancient body memory took on its actual proportions in my skin.

Then Phyllis laughed. "Jesus is here. He wants to give you healing. He is saying, 'Finally'."

First I felt the tears come. Even though this was all completely unbelievable, something in my body grabbed onto Phyllis' words hook line and sinker. Flora taught that in spiritual terms, guilt needs confession and wounds need healing. I was getting both. The pain in my chest softened.

Could I have been a rich young ruler and political assassin? Why not? Could I believe that a compassionate Christ was breaking my historic burden open? Why not? Could I believe that two thousand years could not keep the love of Christ from chasing me until I forgave myself? Why not?

Love didn't stop there. In those moments, I began to heal my unfounded antagonism toward wealthy people. It wasn't money that was my problem; it was that I couldn't trust myself with it. I also began to feel compassion for murderers, plotters, assassins, and deeply fearful people. I was one of them.

Redeemed is a financial word, a word meaning to buy back or make amends for. My sense of worth had been unconsciously tied to my economic ancestry. I had hung onto my debt to Christ by forbidding myself intimacy with money or him for a couple of thousand years. But Christ didn't want my indebtedness. He wanted to play. Somehow he touched my heart and offered me restoration, redemption. He took back the debt and gave me much more. I lost my insidious fear of making money and was soon being befriended by many friends who had inherited wealth, showing me that I could be openhearted, responsible, and loving with financial access.

I had turned to face the strange, infinite, playful, loving Christ and with him said, "Finally."

"I think I am a workaholic," I blurted out to the Northern California head of my denomination. "The more conflict I feel in the church, the harder I work. I don't take breaks. I obsessively count each minute I work." Unhappy, and growing more so, I occasionally felt the right side of my face go numb. I panicked when I thought of my brother's strokes, but felt powerless to change my behaviors. For some reason a counselor suggested that I attend a meeting for adult children of alcoholics. Even though my parents weren't alcoholics, she thought she recognized addiction in me.

A noon meeting was held in a church Sunday school room. Sitting in a kindergartner's chair, I began to put it together that grandfathers and uncles had struggled with alcoholism, gambling, and rage. My parents fought for abstinence. I was twenty-one when they took their first drink.

What was I addicted to? My own adrenalin? Was workaholism a form of physical addiction? Dad ran incessantly, twenty, thirty, a hundred miles at a time. I missed the me that danced, feeling like I took a seriously wrong turn and left her behind.

Recalling the nuclear bomb before the church interview, I met with a therapist in charge of an outpatient treatment program, suddenly fearful that I was about to explode. I was treading upon a landscape of unhealed wounds, traumas, and demons that needed to be disarmed. Dark, inarticulate clouds of sadness, radioactive memories, and messy generational sloughs of parent-child emotions were all mixed up in me. I needed help.

I joined a weekly therapy group and cracked jokes about my own wounds. The therapist accused me of masking my pain. Frankly, I knew it was critical to create fun in misery. I wasn't dancing. A sense of humor was all that I had left. Still, I was grateful that therapy taught me that it was OK to get angry, protect myself, and to duck if someone psychically stabbed and sucked energy from me.

Bravely, I took two months off from church to test out solitude and silence. Upon return, the woman who'd said, "We never have any conflict in church," started growling and cowering Sundays after worship. Like wolf dog Christ, I tried running alongside her with understanding. She ran in the other direction. If I dodged her traps and refused to react, her growling intensified. I felt powerless. She instigated secret meetings, rallied disillusionment about our ministry, and invited the former pastor to dinners that we were not invited to attend. In no time, the whole congregation writhed in stress. I was in awe of the damage one small woman could do.

Talk! The leader of the congregation, an aerospace manager, cornered me in the church parking lot. He talked and talked at me, trying to get me to do something. Stephen and I talked about church over dinner, in the car, and when we woke up. Church conflict was eating us alive. We had to make new rules. No talking about church in bed or in the bathroom. Talk led nowhere. It only exacerbated the mysterious anguish that was haunting everyone.

This is when I began to seriously question the whole idea of church pastoring. This couldn't be what Christ intended, one person leading others without joy, dance, or offering their true self. What did I want? What did I love? What should I pray for? A friend sent me an old prayer. "May those that love us, love us, and those that don't love us, may God turn their hearts. And if God doesn't turn their hearts may he turn their ankles so we'll know them by their limping." It didn't seem like a very good prayer for a pastor. On the other hand, maybe a pastor wrote it.

When the church treasurer, a faithful, strong twenty year member resigned and withdrew her membership, we visited her. She just shook her head and said, "I wouldn't want your job. Ministry is the hardest job in the world." I felt abandoned. Why didn't anybody tell me that the real job of a clergyperson is just trying to love and forgive those we serve?

Seeking any remnant of hope in my religious disaster zone, I turned back to the things that brought me grace: dancing, playing, creating, laughing at what I could, and vacationing with Stephen. If I was going to dance with demons, I didn't have to make it a marathon.

The liturgical colors of Lent are penitential purple, but by our third year in parish ministry they were a freaked-out scarlet. The man appointed as chair of the pastoral relations committee, whose tenure at church was shorter than ours, surveyed five church members. He asked them to grade us on our preaching, visiting, outreach, and administration. The five people chosen were the same elders who agreed I should not dance. Lets just say they didn't give us any A's. Without a word to us about any of it, the chairman gave our report card to the board. We were in shock and even the most avid supporters hobbled around, as confused and dejected as we were. We furiously read books, called in communication, prayer, and ministry specialists. Nothing helped.

On the highest holy day of Christendom, Easter morning, our sanctuary became the empty tomb. Half of the congregation vanished without a word. If I believed in the rapture I'd have thought it had come, but it was not the rapture. Looking out at dozens of empty chairs my heart broke.

In the post Easter weeks Stephen and I ran after the missing bodies like disciples bereft of Jesus. Stephen's chest shot pain. I was tired all the time. We wanted to quit, but the regional minister warned us to wait until we had a plan. He sent us to a center for ministry and career counseling to vomit up the last three years or struggle. Gaining some clarity, we prepared to leave. Relief was on its way.

It was not the end of the world. I never believed that ministry was my ultimate destination. But what the hell? How sad to find reassurance in a 1989 church periodical for women in ministry, *The Daughter's of Clara Newsletter*. "One out of three pastors said, 'Being in the ministry is clearly a hazard to my family.' One of three feels burned out within the first three years of ministry. 90% feel that they were not adequately trained to cope with the demands put on them. 75% have reported a significant crisis due to stress at least once in their ministry. 40% have reported a serious conflict with a parishioner at least once a month."

Career tests confirmed that both Stephen and I should be in the arts. I was more than ready. Stephen couldn't even imagine it. He had only dated and married artists, never actually been one. Instead, he turned his part-time work as a convalescent hospital chaplain into a full-time job.

Visiting parishioners to make our good-byes, I sat in the living room across from a retired pediatrician who had never said too much to me. I only knew that he influenced the church through his tithes. With teacup in hand, he looked me in the eye for the first time and gave me his final benediction. He asked, "Who ordained you? Dancing doesn't belong in the church. I didn't think our church ordained people like you."

I was never more relieved. Finally someone said it right out loud. I looked up at the painting behind his head of round-breasted female dancers cavorting on his living room wall and bestowed on him some of my last words as a parish minister. "Your church ordained me," I said. I did not throw his tea service at him.

3 | Chasing the Dance of Life

Once in awhile one meets people who have crossed an
invisible line, stepping into territory from which there is
no turning back; they are already in such trouble that
nothing they say will make it any better. They are
relaxed and open and they laugh. —ADAM HOUSCHILD

TURNING TO FACE MY FUTURE, I reaffirmed a dancing path
and claimed the credo of Ted Shawn, Ruth St. Denis' partner.

I believe that dance is the oldest,
noblest and most cogent of the arts
I believe that dance is the most perfect symbol
of the activity of God and his angels.
I believe that dance has the power to heal,
mentally and physically.
I believe that true education in the art of dance
is education of the whole person.
I believe that dance is the universal language
and as such has the power to promote one world.
I believe that dance is a way of life which will lead humanity
into continually higher and greater dimensions of existence.

People told me how happy I looked when I organized workshops
called "Wisebodies." Then, six summers before, Phil and I led a

dance week at Pacific School of Religion. Folks from around the country who would never make dance their vocation came to move, pray, and partake of the dancing body, in love with a thing they couldn't shake: group love and a wisdom born of the dance of life. My art, care for people, and playfulness gracefully converged during these sacred dance weeks. Everything worked. I knew who I was and where I belonged. The only problem was it only lasted for one week a year. At the end of the week the dancing people evaporated into the San Francisco fog, leaving just the seminary, a Golden Gate view, Phil and me. It felt like Brigadoon. But, Brigadoon wasn't enough anymore.

Exiting my church job and choosing to be an artist meant running headlong into the entrepreneurial wilderness. Thank God I didn't know how big the wilderness was and thank God for Phil, probably the closest I could ever come to having one of those TV angels who is always there shaking a head, laughing, and offering counter intuitive suggestions to his more high strung associate.

A handsome guy with white-bread roots, Phil's an adult child of normal parents. His Hoosier dad was a business professor and his mom, a gem with a biblical name, Dorcas. Anytime you ask him how he is, he says, "I'm fine," and means it. Half of the world can relate to his sensible shoes and boardroom composure. He makes the two of us look slightly more grown up.

After Judith departed for New York Phil said to me, "I am going to follow you." I couldn't believe it. I danced from drama to drama as he lay back on wooden dance floors, apparently unconcerned about my stability. He had a right to his own dramas, but didn't play them out. As a ringleader in gay church culture, having been married and divorced once, his loyalty was powerful. It was not born from pre-scriptions, but from his mix of freedom, principled goodness, and love.

Being Mr. Mild Mannered is Phil's disguise for being an ecstatic revolutionary living in an inner city Oakland loft. As a graphic and textile artist with a MA in Visual Design from UC Berkeley, I fanta-sized him as either a multi-winged seraph or a Tibetan Buddhist go-getter in a past life. This time around he was an insatiable performer, dancer, artist, speaker, poet, writer, theologian, magna-cum-laude-honorable, off the scale introvert. Once, when asked to bring a walking stick to a dance conference Phil made a one-of-a-kind urban walking stick out of six feet of Rebar, a jangle of CDs, floppy disks, hand-dyed fabric tassels and feathers, hung from a giant gear. Too shy to actually carry it around, I used it. Phil was my other wing.

*

Spring rain beat down on the window of my Mazda truck at dusk on Highway 101 in California. I was on my way to a conference to meet Stephen. As I listened to an audiotape by Dr. Bernie Siegel describe how he found his spirit guide, I felt something unusual. I turned off the tape deck. Hydroplaning across sheets of water through Gilroy, the garlic capital of the world, right out loud I asked, "Who's there?"

"Mary," said a voice without hesitation.

"Mary?" I repeated to myself, digging through old inner Mary files. Mother of Jesus? Mary Magdalene, Mary? What other Mary's do I know? I didn't have particularly strong Mary beliefs. Do Catholic icons talk to Protestants?

My throat popped tight as I realized I was having a literal conversation with a "voice." Two choices stood before me. Decide I was crazy and stop the whole thing. Or go wide-eyed into the conversation as if I'd been waiting for it my whole life.

Having heard voices before, I put my bets on being called crazy. "What do you want?" I asked.

"I have something to tell you, but it is hard to swallow."

How did she know I had a knot in my throat? "What is it?" I questioned.

Then, very bluntly she said seven unforgettable words, "You are going to have a baby."

I didn't even know that these were words I ached to hear. Married nine years, with no children, and no intense need to have any, all at once I knew that to have a baby was to love life more than I ever had. A small dam in my heart cracked.

I cried for the next hundred miles as excitement climbed up from my belly. I couldn't wait to tell Stephen. Finding him at the conference, I dragged him outside, jumping, jumping, jumping, until I could say the words, "I'm going to have a baby!" I was thirty-three years old and as full of joy as any newly pregnant mom. I told him about the voice, never pausing to consider how peculiar it sounded or what it might mean for him. Stephen Joseph Winton-Henry didn't flinch. A Joseph to my Mary, he held me and took it in.

Madeleine L'Engle wrote, "This is the season of irrational wild where love blooms hot and wild. If Mary had been full of reason there would not have been any room for the child." Stephen and I were ready for something wild and new.

Unfortunately, Mary didn't know one important fact. We were infertile. We had attended infertility seminars to learn about tests, food, surgeries, medicine, and tubes. Friends had divulged secret ways to get pregnant. I pulled out my fertility doll from West Africa. We changed our diets, got acupunctured, had surgery, took herbs and vitamins, and give up sugar. No baby.

Truthfully, I knew that hearing a voice isn't any stranger than trying to make a baby in a doctor's office. At our first infertility appointment we showed up "ready to conceive."

"Do you have the sample?" asked the nurse at the desk, looking busy and slightly accusatory.

We looked at each other like two surprised virgins. "We didn't know we were supposed to bring anything," we said.

"What? You were supposed to collect the semen at home. Oh well, take room 32," the nurse said with annoyance, handing us something like a Tupperware snack cup.

There we were, Lucille Ball and Ricky Ricardo trying to make whoopee on a gynecological table with a crooked orange seascape tacked to the ceiling above. We tried turning out the lights, various positions, together, alone, but emerged sweaty, grumpy and spermless.

After months of appointments that involved poking, pulling, and the same crooked seascape, I never befriended one medical personnel. Shouldn't babies be conceived in the love of relationships? Where was my village, my midwife?

"I am going to scrape your cervix, Honey. This won't hurt."

"Ouch!"

"Doctor, I am a holistic person! Isn't having a baby supposed to be a spiritual experience?" Shrugging, he handed me a support group brochure.

"Ouch."

As I got these modern day Immaculate Conception processes figured out, I would enter a tiny exam room, hold Stephen's hand, and lay down with my feet in the air, staring up at a crooked seascape. Again, the doctor would say, "This won't hurt," and stick a syringe up me farther than he should. Afterwards, I would lavish myself with bouquets of baby's breath as consolation.

One day after our insemination appointment Stephen and I left in separate cars. Before we could rendezvous, he had a car accident. When I found him he was headed back to emergency in an ambulance. Hospitals seemed less and less hospitable to new life. This was never clearer than the day that the doctor and nurse argued about staff work schedules while I was being inseminated. That settled it. I knew that my baby was not going to come through a syringe.

I was both grieved and relieved. I didn't feel a strong pull to be swollen, big boobed, or labor in pain. I was more interested in "having" a baby than making one. Adoption was the answer.

Stephen and I started playing adoption hopscotch, jumping from county adoption meetings to foster adoption, from international adoption orientations to homes for unwed mothers, from books on private adoption to circulating a letter about us to anyone who might know someone who needed to place their child with adoptive parents. Embarrassed, I only mailed one.

Holding onto Mary's voice, I told people all over the United States that I was looking for a baby. It was in Indiana, where Phil and I were to lead a workshop at a Mennonite Church, that our hosts, Ben and Susan asked me, "Do you have children?"

"I hope to adopt," I said almost nonchalantly.

Susan said, "You know, my brother-in-law is a doctor in a clinic. I could tell him you are looking."

Their kindness and hospitality was so natural it might have been the first time I felt genuine hope about becoming a mother. But, that night it wasn't a baby that filled my dreams. It was the growth of InterPlay. I saw classes, a publishing company, and a leadership program. In the pitch dark I woke up and wrote down the picture that had popped into my night vision. Goshen Indiana, it seemed, was a fertile place.

With one foot and most of my spirit out the church door, I invited twelve acquaintances to a workshop on improvisation. Phil was present. Out of those who attended, Phil and I claimed Leo Keegan and Debra Weir as the first members of a performance company we called Wing It! Performance Ensemble. It was a flighty name heralding an unstoppable drive to reintegrate body, spirit, and humor through improvisation.

We taught our first InterPlay classes in the Unitarian church hall where legendary Isadora Duncan once debuted. Isadora said, "You were once wild here. Don't let them tame you." I was counting on that.

I loved working with Phil. Thrusting toward my visions; I leapt off improvisational cliffs like a bungee-cord jumper, discovering whole new ways of looking at the world. Meanwhile Phil turned the world right side up again and helped people get to the same places by taking a ladder. He decoded my ideas into usable, charismatic forms and often came up with better ones.

Amusement shot through our veins. Improvising was a drug. All I had to do was glance at Phil to know he was completely there. At first we were like positive ends of two magnets. Pushing through the force field between us we turned into hysterical twelve-year-olds, breaking the barrier of ordinary time, utterly confident in our ability to make dances on the spot. Each time we ended and bowed, we knew. The audience knew. Two unrehearsed trapeze artists had swung into space and caught each other in effortless, synchronous magic.

Our collaboration caused people to assume we were married. But ours was not a love anyone could define. Neither Phil nor I have ever been able to articulate what we are to each other. While events and mysterious voices may lead to joy, Phil, a person who catalyzes happiness, is an unimaginable gift.

As if I wasn't lucky enough, each night I pulled into my driveway and went inside to find Stephen sprawled on the green sofa in front of the TV. Together, watching a show, sharing highlights from our day and getting in bed, I relaxed and let go of zeal. I was home.

Our last day as co-pastors of the church was Thanksgiving Sunday. At the turkey dinner, (no pun intended), Stephen and I were given our go-away-for-good present: two tickets to the Civic Light Opera and one pair of small opera glasses. Was it a sign? Our sights were set on something more entertaining if we could get help to clarify our vision. Right then and there, I determined that I would always put the Dance of Life first. But first I had to heal.

I had danced where one shouldn't and refrained from dancing where there should be holy polkas. Fully flaming dancing reverend, I ached for a divine dance with love like a junior high girl. Caught in a stink of being a double-breasted dancer, was I tricked or was I the trickster? Perhaps, for the church I was no prayer, but maybe, still, someday, someone's answer to it.

Stephen and I turned in our church keys, refinanced our house, and flew to Paris for Christmas. Hosts of angels welcomed us. Each time they appeared on a cathedral portal or Parisian monument my heart leapt. But the Winged Victory of Samothrace took my breath. Her air-splitting torso and defiant arc of wing marked an utterly new season. It was my season of wings. An angel was with me, but not of the Hallmark variety. Mine was a thrusting, ambitious angel. She wanted to dance. She wanted to create. She wanted to fly and could care less about propriety or being taken seriously. She was bent on a whole new life.

Stephen and I did Europe as happy paupers, bedding down in cheap hotels. On Christmas Eve we ate Vietnamese food, hung up our stockings, and wound up a miniature, dancing Christmas tree. In the morning we gifted each other with chocolate and bah humbug socks. But, inside my stocking there was one more present: a note from Stephen that read, "This year, a child."

Christmas day we took a train to Chartres Cathedral and entered just as the chords of the organ bid farewell to a small congregation gathered for mass. In one corner stood a case enshrining a blue snatch of Mary's veil. I mused about the devotion to relics such as these as I sat with Stephen on a wicker chair in the nave. Bundling my coat around me to fend off the December cold, I observed an old man depart from mass. He walked down the long center aisle, stopped midway facing the door, his back to the altar and crossed himself. I nudged Stephen. The old guy was facing the wrong way. After the man left, I got up to see where he had stopped. In the floor, mid-aisle, I saw the rose shaped pattern.

Gongs hit my memory. It was the labyrinth. I completely forgot that Chartres was one of a dozen cathedrals with this circuitous dance path in the nave floor. Since the twelfth century labyrinths were used for Easter vigil dances. Traveling the labyrinth on your knees was an alternate to making a pilgrimage to the Holy Land.

For me, finding the labyrinth was like discovering Atlantis or a lost relic. Here was visible evidence of the dancing God, all forty by forty feet of it, now covered by row upon row of chairs. Were the old man and I the only ones who knew of the mythic treasure lying beneath our feet? There was only one brochure about it entitled "The Mystery of the Labyrinth." It confessed total ignorance about the labyrinth's purpose. A footprint of the dance of life filled the cathedral, yet there was almost no memory of a dancing faith. Still, I knew the labyrinth was sign and signature of the body at prayer, a soul map of people dancing their spiritual path.

The angel inside me jumped up and down, nodding emphatically, "Yes, yes." She dashed back and forth between my heart, the rose in the center of the labyrinth, and the brilliant Chartres rose window.

※

Home from Europe I was surprised by an invitation to attend a labyrinth ceremony at Holy Names College in Oakland. Apparently, the labyrinth was resurrecting itself in the dreams of North American mystics like Joan Macmillan. Joan had chalked out the Chartres labyrinth on a classroom floor, making it possible for a hundred people to take their own journey to the center of the rose. When I stepped onto the path, I burst into laughter. Having just left a painful ministry, it was like taking a cosmic antacid. Hilarity burbled up. My angel went wild. She didn't care. Even though everyone else was in a reverent trance, I skipped like Dorothy off to see the Wizard of Oz.

Stephen and I began getting adoption nibbles. A friend called to inform us that a woman was giving birth in Guatemala. Were we interested? For twenty-four hours we sweated about the expense, the legal work, and the emotional demands of going to Latin America. Was this our baby? With nothing but pre-school Spanish we decided to forego that route.

Mid-March, in the midst of not worrying about babies at all, I answered the kitchen phone. A man introduced himself as a lawyer from Goshen, Indiana. Almost as bluntly as Mary announcing, "You're going to have a baby," the lawyer asked, "Are you still interested in an adoption?"

I stuttered, "Yes!" and the lawyer went on to say that he had a client who was pregnant and needed to find a home for a baby that was on the way. She was 39, single, had grown children and was recovering from several difficult relationships.

My womb flip-flopped. Indiana was holy in a funny way. It was the birth state of my father, grandfather, many Wintons, and me. It was Phil's home state and the headquarters of the church that ordained me. It seemed more than good fortune that I was scheduled to fly there for two professional meetings in upcoming months. My tickets were paid for. I only had to rent a car to meet the lawyer and his client at his office in downtown Goshen.

The minute I walked into the room, Louise and I connected. Our faces, our eyes, were alike. Were we cousins? Recognition crackled between us. Louise was earthy, practical, and definitely Christian.

Across the law office table she spoke her truth in soft, clear words. "I could never have an abortion. God wants me to find the right people to care for this baby. I just know this is what God wants." She said it more than once, making herself strong enough to do the impossible thing she was about to do.

I gave her a small photo album full of pictures of our house, our parents, and us. She took them. The silent bond that we planted in each other, mother to mother was the only hope either of us could cling to. Everything else was faith and grace.

We met again on a June trip that for the second time coincided with a prescheduled, professional meeting. Stephen joined me. After spending a night in Chicago he and I drove to an 11:00 a.m. meeting at the lawyer's office trying not to ask the lurking question, "Would she change her mind?"

Speeding down the interstate, a road sign told us we were crossing from Illinois to Indiana. Stephen flashed, "Doesn't the time change between Illinois and Indiana?"

I gasped, "We're late!" Panic bit me with all the force of an irrational mother protecting her young. I was warding off a miscarriage. We veered off the highway to alert the lawyer. "We're going to be late!" I trembled.

Even after arriving an hour late, Louise was waiting at the lawyer's office. The physical burden of pregnancy and the difficulty of her decision marked her face. Miraculously she was firm in her resolve in spite of family members who wanted the child. She said, "God is calling me to find a family for this baby. I know you are the ones."

Sunday August 5, 1990, at 9:00 a.m. the phone rang. It was neither doctor, lawyer, nor adoption agency, but Susan, our Mennonite friend in Goshen. She said, "A little girl has been born." It had been nine months since Stephen put his prophetic note in my Christmas stocking.

Both the doctor and lawyer suggested we get Katie in two days. That morning I attended a church where milk and honey were offered along with bread and juice. I took the milk, praying for my own nurture and that of the tiny baby who had fought an umbilical cord wrapped around her neck and much more to find her way to us. Stephen and I called her Katherine Emily, Katie-Em.

Tuesday morning at the airport ticket counter a blue-suited man looked up at us mildly and told us the plane was full. "Would you be interested in taking a later flight?" he asked.

Lurching forward, I said too loudly, "No! We're getting our baby!" I had never known myself to be this anxious. Motherhood was not going to be easy.

The man stiffened. When Stephen quickly explained about our adoption the airline employee offered, "In that case, would you like to fly first class?"

Within minutes I was drinking champagne with a new diaper bag under my feet and Grandma Lurley's just-crocheted baby afghan on my lap. I couldn't believe there was this much grace. Destiny wrapped us in bright, gentle wings and carried us to our child.

On the ground, a full moon lit the way as we sped toward the hospital from Chicago to Goshen. At 11 p.m., only the emergency room door was open. We called the lawyer and waited for him in the lobby. In five minutes both he and the doctor who delivered Katie came and waited with us. Upstairs, Katie's birth mother said good-bye to her baby one last time and then asked to see us. Taking the elevator up to the maternity ward, the ride intensified the lightness in my head. The door opened. From the nursing station spoked a dozen small white rooms. Following the doctor, Stephen and I found Louise in room 212. She was crying in heaving sobs as she somehow told us, "All my children are special, but this one really is. I have been singing to her. Her brother and sister have been here to say good-bye. She's so beautiful."

Her grief was inconsolable. She knew it. I knew it. I cried too. It was all we could do. Those six or seven minutes sealed our lives in an eternal contract. We were both mother to this baby. We both leapt our natural instincts of female territoriality to offer this child a transcendent love. If humility is a feeling, that's what I felt when I sat with Louise. I made no attempt at closure.

Stephen and I were escorted to a room three doors down. A nurse carried in a little blanketed thing, put her tiny body in my arms, and said, "Here is your daughter."

> *Shock of joy*
> *little face*
> *love-bursting*
> *born to these*

unaccustomed arms
at midnight still
holding you
and each other
as angel song
explodes from the
heart of the world,
"She's born! She's come!"
Mary's word
flesh at last.

For the next two weeks Stephen, Katie, and I stayed with Ben and Susan on their farm. They gave us a suite, a baby bath and cradle, and a view of green woods, a pond, and a barn. No stinky manger for us. Susan held us with the warmth of the Great Mother. We slept a lot and took our first walks through cornfields, Amish gardens, and clotheslined side yards. We had no house to clean, no food to buy. Mennonite church and InterPlay friends brought us dinners and invited us to their homes.

Grace enthusiastically sheltered us. We had a village. We had Katie. In a world named "Struggle," where pain and stress regulate most of what is known about life how could there be this much grace? I was confounded yet not surprised. There had been the voice. There had been the voice.

I left the church wanting more than ever to love God and belong to a dancing people.

"Give it up!" yelled a pragmatist in my brain. "American institutions—seminaries, churches, governments, health care, businesses—won't dance. It takes dancing people to make dancing institutions."

Deep disappointments in the church and myself lumped up.

In a dream, I saw a bowling ball roll down the street ahead of me. It had a will of its own. It was my fate and it was on a roll. I chased it as it rolled consciously up to the glass doors of a high-rise office building. Knowing the business world had absolutely no use for dance, I picked up the ball and threw it back towards the street. When it returned to the building like a magnet, I opened the door and it made a left turn down one corridor and a hard right down another. It knew where it was going. My fate rolled up to an office door and waited. A woman in a suit opened the door.

I couldn't imagine myself in a suit, much less an office. The only thing I knew about power was people dancing, hands joined, stepping left, stepping right, over and over, awe and delight radiating from their faces. I had to follow what made me happy. I had to dance.

It dawned on me that turning away from the church, my work would be no easier. Whether destined to dance with business, health care, or education, the bowling ball of fate led me toward an oddly configured lifestyle. Chances were that something would get bowled off its base. Probably me.

Again, I wondered why people refuse to dance their lives. From my great repertoire of crackpot theories, I consoled myself with one of my favorites: I call it the curse of the touchy-feely dragon. I suspect that a touchy-feely dragon secretly haunts and terrifies western people, particularly men. It was either that or our bodies are so powerful it is essential to repress them.

My imagination went wild with the theory. I saw it all. Each night, CEO's roll over in their sleep, the corporate offices are locked up, their dream body flinches as a dragon tail hurtles in their direction. Back at their office, with midnight security turned on, the danger is alarmingly real. Out from under boardroom tables the hidden dragon emerges.

She snivels, howls, and oozes a strange golden juice. On tremendous hind legs she dances, hips swinging and knocking abstract art off the walls. Expanding to full height the glass ceiling rattles as her hysteria devours all sign of reason. Making her nightly track through the home offices, she leaves trails of instinct, intuition, emotion, silliness, and all manner of stupid questions. Eventually she comes upon a lone man or woman at their desk under a solitary light.

Hearing the pounding, not sure if it is his heart, the man opens the door to see her enormous head dip down. He stares, frozen, hearing his name as sensuously spoken as any lover and knows he is about to lose sanity, future, security, all sense of himself. An electric, slimy, buzzing eel ignites his spine until he senses nothing but his name. The terrifying creature nuzzles, breathes on him, and then eats him alive.

Taking flight, she leaps off of the building, a shadow in the sleeping sky. As she beats her wings, she spits out his remains on the usual heaps: spiritual centers, art studios, mountain cabins, psychiatric and addiction units, ashrams, and psychic institutes.

In the morning the touchy-feely dragon flies back to the boardroom where no one expects to find her. She dances on the table one more time before crawling below to sleep at the feet of her patrons, satiated by the feast.

"What a waste," the man's cronies say the next day. But, every night they fear that they might be next to be taken as sacrifice. Sometimes it's a man, sometimes a woman, a small price for the collective refusal to touch and feel.

How could I wear a suit?

Recommitted to bringing dance and religion together I agreed to lead twelve Presbyterian clergywomen at a Santa Fe retreat center. They were weary and I knew why. Many had been the first women to lead churches. They bore scars and in some cases had been publicly shunned. Our days together confirmed that this was the right work for me. When we were invited to attend the Cochiti Indian Harvest Dance I was doubly rewarded.

Chatter filled the van as we peeled through the New Mexico desert toward buildings that seemed stuck out in the middle of nowhere. Lines of parked cars, vendor stalls and game booths bordering the pueblo gave no indication of the mystery awaiting us. We walked between two earth brown buildings and headed toward the sound of drums and deep male voices pulsing from within a sacred kiva chamber. The spirit of prayer was palpable. It was just beyond this

that a great circle of dancers filled the plaza. Hundreds of pe⟨
in folding chairs bought from Woolworths and Kmart. No one
spoke, except tourists. Elegantly costumed children, men, and
women carried banners that pierced the sky. Their feet spoke rhythmically to the white ground beneath them. Huge drums grounded
the dance as people sang back with the voice of the dance.

An old man threw a sharp eye toward chatty tourists as if to say,
"Shhh, we're praying." An old emptiness in me ached. It was a hole
in my chest the shape of a drum that no one played anymore.
Remembering Africa, I was struck that even though this was
America, it felt like an utterly different continent from the one I
knew. Emotion stuck in my throat, thighs, and sternum. Seeing
these dancers, I knew what a great distance it was to take my own
people to the Promised Land. Why didn't God give up? Why didn't
I? I heard the lament of the Dancing God.

> *I weep for you*
> *my people.*
> *You dance only in your dreams,*
> *dreams you forget.*
>
> *You speak of hunger.*
> *You do not know*
> *the ache in your chest is where*
> *dance was ripped out of you.*
>
> *Do you not know my loneliness for you?*
> *How utterly you have fallen asleep,*
> *dimmed by word on word,*
> *chasms between thought and action.*
>
> *Without me your joy is small.*
> *Your life is small.*
> *Your vigor wanes.*
> *Your communities suffer.*

You confine me to bars,
privatize me, mock me,
exile me to the periphery,
robbing my power to create you.

Even your children despise me,
They are visionless and disrespectful.
They do not raise up
for their elders are motionless.

Where is the Festal Dance?
Abandoned!
Gangs seize the ground where
drum and sweat brought me life.

You stripped skin from the drum,
put your foot through the timbrel,
shouted down the dance from the pulpit.
You strapped yourself to the pew.

You outlawed the old ways:
circle dances, nature songs, fertility rites,
criminalized the dance of
"heathens" and slaves.

You forgot that I AM a Dancing God.

I am in the fury of those contesting you
dancing all night in the heat:
youth, underpaid immigrants
outcasts, addicts, human trash.

I am in the hidden places of dance
resurrected, reborn,
dancers with dancers,
lost in sweat, beat, and pulse.

I am in circles where blood pounds
energy out of energy,
whole truth, whole wisdom
foot, pelvis, heart, face.

Dead in you, I dance in Hawaiian
West African, Cochiti Indian.
My tears flowing without end
Among those who pray to dance.

My people?
Will you not dance again?
Your rituals are all sorrow.
Without me you will not be moved.

I was tempted to run off and join a more body-friendly culture. I could find Hula, Tai Chi, Baharata Natyam, or African Dance anywhere in the San Francisco area. When I read Anne Cameron's *Daughters of Copperwoman* I ached for companionship like those shared by the native women she knew. But, it seemed like anytime I turned away from my WASPy roots I received a shamanistic taboo like the one at the end of her book that read,

> *Anyone who appropriates these stories by retelling or adapting them is betraying the trust in which they were offered. Look instead into your own history/herstory: what you need is in the stories of your sisters, mothers, aunts, grandmothers, foremothers. Search for it: then write it, sing it, paint it, dance it and share it.*

What was my story? I hardly knew the names of my great grandparents. Yet, Anne Cameron's words seemed more than a casual threat. If I was to follow the wisdom of my body, my people, my spiritual legacy, I had to "search for it: then write it, sing it, paint it, dance it and share it." With no story to draw on, I did the only thing I could do. I danced. Slowly, dancing helped me realize what had happened. All I had to do was look deeply into what was right before my eyes.

I put down my foot
I send out my voice
I jump, fall
bent over
an old woman
a beat-up bum
a soldier
a purple-tongued hag.

I put down my foot
bring blood to my palms
clapping, stomping,
singing out my brains
seeing others play
stomping, whipping around,
slapping mud with their hands
making little worlds.

We do it together.
Heat rises.
Everything ugly sparkles.
The glint.
I can see it.
Low tide and high tide
in every piece of matter
Spirit.
In everything made,
Spirit.
In every body,
Spirit.
In the air,
Spirit.
Asleep and awake,
Spirit.
I can see it.
I can see it.

Can't see it?
Don't die with that lie.
Spirit registers
in every sense,
lances the solar plexus,
climbs the spine,
travels lip to lip,
chest to chest,
glance to glance,
in turbulence and tenderness.

Who said Spirit
would only feel good?
Spirit stings.
Spirit dances truth in
every art
laugh
flinch
thought
rainfall
word
street
building.

Normal
as a fly,
as a human,
or a waltzing world,
look and see
it's in the center of your eye,
this Spirit dance.

My angel knew exactly where she was going. Crashing through
the unknown on a bucking bronco, happy as a goose, she threw

glances over her shoulder on a regular basis to see if I was still following. The more I followed, the more inventive she became. Why not teach entire groups of stodgy Americans to manifest corporate dreams without excessive five-year plans, studies, and surveys? I knew that if I could find the body logic that could unify a group's spirit and let people fly, not just as one, but as a collective, then some significant change might occur in the way westerners do things.

There were few improvisational dance companies in San Francisco. None that also sang and spoke. While no respectable theater artist would admit anything close to Judeo-Christian spirituality, Phil and I did what many feared. We flew by the seat of our pants, threw ourselves on the wings of the moment, entertained our tradition, and invited the critics. Improvising was ecstatic when it worked, and made me tight when it didn't. But, ecstasy trumped our failures.

Phil and I honed Wing It! performances to be as cohesive as rehearsed groups. The highest complement was always an incredulous audience member who said, "No, really, that was improvised?"

For our first major concert, "God, Sex, and Power," we rented an avant-garde dance hall in San Francisco's Mission District and shaped the concert like a liturgy full of sexual energy. Opening night one critic came. The lights went up and I walked onstage to invoke the dream.

> *Here's an idea.*
> *Let us make something out of nothing.*
> *No not nothing.*
> *Let us gather up everything that we ever were or are or will be.*
> *Let us be Shapers,*
> *Creators,*
> *Makers,*
> *of Some Thing.*
> *Some World,*
> *Some Living.*
> *Let us dare to succeed at it,*
> *Dare to fail at it,*
> *Dare to fly on the wings of this moment.*

Let us improvise our dreams.
Let us leap boldly from the shoulders of our lives,
Our histories,
Our loves,
Our disasters.

Here's an idea.
Let us play ourselves out!
(The real work)
Let us do nothing at all.
It may not matter.
Let us run the risk of naked individuality.
Let us go out wildly
Not just as one,
But as a union, an ensemble.

Here is an idea.
When we make our worlds
Let us commit to them
hold still with them
let them go when it is time.
Let us breathe,
Let us sing,
Let us laugh,
Let us dance,
Let us see what will be
when we invoke
God, Sex, and Power.

A PSR friend, Elaine Kirkland put her hands to the keyboard, chanting, "Something, nothing, maybe everything, wild holy power. Leaping, laughing, dancing, chancing, flyyyyyy awayyyyyy."

There was an earthquake that night. At the end of the performance the audience cheered. But the critic had a grumpy night and critiqued our self-indulgence. I took refuge on my sofa, plagued by serious questions about what I was doing. In spite of the bad review, my love affair with Wing It's irreverent saints of the body propelled me forward. They were strange people who clung to knowledge of flight, and refused to forsake their hunger for either heaven or earth: Debra, Leo, Beth, John, David, Masankho, Amar, Penny, Scott, Julie, Loretta, Freider, Susan, Ted. My dancing village was finally a weekly community.

We performed throughout the Bay Area in questionable neighborhoods, using grand themes like "Fear and Abandon;" "Life and Death;" "Now What Do I Do? Transition, Anxiety, and Change;" and "Too Much Fun!" In some ways I had come a long way from that first dance in college, "War and Peace." But, in other ways, I was still obsessed with fundamental, grandiose themes and with being very, very, unbelievably human.

The church that ordained me invited me to dance in worship on World Communion Sunday. I looked forward to seeing the good people in the beautiful sanctuary surrounded by oaks. On that morning I dressed in white and gathered many kinds of bread. After I processed in with them, lifting a beautiful loaf, I spoke a few poetic words. I had not been in church for a year, yet my soul was still completely rooted in Christianity, the Bible, liturgy, my lineage, my ancestral dance. I was still ordained.

Two weeks later a woman from the church called. After my dance a man said to her, "Did you see those nipples dancing around the sanctuary?" She alerted the female minister who said that women ministers have to be careful to wear clothes that are not too revealing.

Decades of angst erupted, from having my teenage arabesque shunned at the altar, to the consequences of portraying that offending whore, Babylon, the braless white horse, Eve dancing with a common garden snake, or even performing fully robed in a Pentecostal processional. I wanted to yell, "NIPPLES? What about the damn dance? Did he notice that I was praying?" Instead my teeth clamped. I hung up and flew to my computer with Vesuvius rage,

"Did you see those nipples dancing around the sanctuary?"
What a line.
Leading worship one day
at my church of ten years
me the dancing proclaimer
brought in bread
earthy stuff
to the communion table to celebrate
all these types of people
all these types of bread.
My nipples must have gotten hard.
I wear size 32A.
Always have been small breasted
No need for a bra.
Of course as a minister
I take care not to be too revealing.

"Did you see those nipples dancing around the sanctuary?"
The female church minister told her,
"Even if it does me and my sister an injustice
to have to hide ourselves away
we do it.
It is our job."
I think hard about this.
Put on more layers?
I was wearing two shirts at the time.
"Did you see those nipples dancing around the sanctuary?"
So I learn the real purpose of bras
to bandage the nipple
wrap away nurture.
Nipples, how sexual!
I am told, "It is not a problem
anywhere but church,
I dress that way myself."
Take care not to get hard

God should not arouse us
excite us. But,
part of me is glad my 32A's get some attention at last.

More than that I know
Nipples should be dancing in every sanctuary.
Nipples are Holy.
God nurturing.
An original source of sustenance.
They are glorious in cultures.
They are simply there.
Everyday reminders that women are.
Women are.
Women are.
Women are holy.
Women are good.
Women are sexual.
Women's body is holy ground.
World communion.
Offering the primal meal
The meal that is truly timeless
The suckle.
I will put milk on the communion table from now on.
Breasts and tits flying wildly around sanctuaries
as it should be.
"Did you see those nipples dancing around the sanctuary?"
In a scared church
in a male church
in a church afraid of women's bodies
in a church revolted by nipples
severely revolted by thighs and crotches
We are reminded, men and women,
that there will be no getting hard in church.
If you get hard keep it to yourself.
Metal codpieces, polyester bras.

"Did you see those nipples dancing around the sanctuary?"
And the people said, "No."
Said the children innocently, "No, Mommy."
Nipples don't belong in church.
Let us not suckle our children there
or call attention to our real bodies.
Let us pretend that only gauzy angels dance
and that our body is asexual.
Just a woman.
Just a man.
Forever more they will ask
"Did you see those nipples dancing around the sanctuary?"
and the people will say
"No."

Phil and I traveled to Sydney, Australia to teach. The first night as I lay down to sleep I remembered to ask Jesus' assistance in the coming days. As I closed my eyes to pray, suddenly a passionate, hard French kiss leapt off the screen of my unruly imagination and onto my lips. My eyes flipped open, lids tensed. Talk about in your face. What the devil? Christ respects boundaries, doesn't he?

In the morning, preparing to lead a retreat on embodied prayer, Phil and I brainstormed questions to ask participants. Phil suggested we ask them, "What is the cutting edge of your prayer life?" Then he turned to me. "What's your cutting edge?"

I blushed, trying to shove back the memory of Christ's intrusive kiss. Then in typical fashion and in spite of myself, I spit out, "Being French kissed by Christ." Saying it aloud multiplied my questions. Was this the same Christ who howled with me, danced with me, and healed my murderous guilt?

The retreat wasn't as interesting or challenging as my own query. When it was over I went to the home of a dear friend. Trish Delaney welcomed me at her door and invited me in to sit at her kitchen table. I loved her elfin spirit. As a former nun, she was unpretentiously doused in divine mystery, had intimate conversations with Jesus and was a master of silence and touch. She innocently asked, "How are you, Darling?"

I put it right out. "Trish, I think I was French kissed by Christ."

She grinned. By her reaction I guessed that a nun might know about such things. After all, they are married to him. She assured me that this kind of love was as much a part of mysticism as any other, though it was rarely mentioned.

Somehow this both did and didn't reassure me.

Sensing my fatigue, Trish offered to give me a massage. She led me to a room as peaceful as a hermitage and stepped outside while I took off my clothes and lay down on the table. Upon return, with loving hands and oil she anointed me. I relaxed into the healing touch as she put one hand on my belly and one hand on my face. My face felt ravenous for tender touch. I grabbed her hand and pressed her fingers harder into my cheekbones, eye sockets, and jaw. I sucked this touch deep down into the pores of my little human self. Strangely relieved, I settled down. When Trish left the room she invited me to rest as long as I needed.

As I lay in the quiet of the room soothed by music and warm sheets, he of the kiss returned. This time he didn't need to wake me up to show me that divinity will take every path when it comes to love. It was I who was afraid of such powerful intimacy, human or divine. The encounter was exquisite. But how could I speak of it? Only poetry seemed adequate. Mystics like Mechtilde of Magdeburg, Clare of Assisi, Saint Francis, and Teresa of Avila, also consumed by divine love poured out their encounters in theo-poetic rapture. Could I?

Inside candle lit skin
He came, holy ghost
to sing a song so sweet
and sensual as to
anoint sex
in his heavenly arms
and disorderly mystery.
Christ, sex-healer,

if you can make love
then nothing, nothing,
is shameful or wrong
with sex anymore.
Fecund in every cell,
lover of this body,
how can I not
rise from your table
with touch afire?
My hands, blind eyes
see for the first time.

Returning to the States, my hands felt like amputees recently reattached. I immediately enrolled in a massage course called Care Through Touch: The Art of Anointing at the Graduate Theological Union. Nuns and priests were among my classmates. I was not the only religious person that Mystery lured to the feast of Love. Communion was literally at hand. But, instead of one table there were ten, each with a human being on it, all of whom needed a lot of healing when it came to the body. Some of us felt sexually anorexic, having refused the manna of simple physical affection for decades.

With one massage after another the springs of health among my classmates began to flow again. I learned that the words, "Take, eat, this is my body broken for you" was not limited to church or bread.

On the first day of the massage course, Stephen lost his job. He was burnt out, we had no savings, and it was clearly up to me to carry the next leg of our financial burden. I had to make a plan fast. Motivated by fears of being devoured by giant department store cash registers and endless assembly lines, I catapulted into action. I targeted professionals who wanted to develop their body wisdom. Thank God I was no longer terrified of asking for money. I met with two friends and supporters who each granted me $5,000 to get started and hold onto our mortgage. Then, I called hundreds of people and enrolled them in ten new Wisdom of the Body groups.

Three months and thirteen groups later, Jesus was more than my right-hand man. I called on him in classes, theaters, churches, and in the homes of people I counseled. Once afraid of overwhelming Jesus with requests, I didn't understand why more people didn't involve him in their work, especially clergy. Of course, looking back at the intense, imaginative, unorthodox encounters I'd shared with him, I completely understood why people remained mum.

In spite of all the increasing intimacy with Christ, I still questioned whether I was experiencing the truly personal, pervasive life presence other people talked about. Sure we'd recently been through hell together, romanced the stars, and set up shop. But, it still felt like a long distance relationship where I was the needy female always calling her guy on the phone.

One day, driving north from San Jose and gazing at clouds that hung over the automobiles, I asked Jesus, "Shouldn't I feel something more?"

I thought I heard, "I don't want to be used by you. I just want to be with you."

"Be with me?"

My affair with the Divine had grown serious. Was I ready to pray that much? I was too busy dancing. Then again, Jesus loves to dance.

4 | Deep Waters

Dive for dreams though the stars dance backwards and
dance away your death at the wedding.

—EE CUMMINGS

I DON'T KNOW HOW OR WHEN I got enrolled in the great mystery school. Maybe it was when the energy came down into my head years before. Like a kind of Harry Potter, I sensed I was crossing thresholds, landing in alternate worlds where the unbelievable became believable. This school also called for difficult physical tests like the year I call my PhD in death and dying.

It started with suffering from unusually intense fatigue after leading so many body wisdom groups. A friend, Fawn Christianson, offered me a Trager bodywork session. I thought, "Sure!" She knew how to rock the water in your body to release its healing power. Crawling onto her table, I smiled uncomfortably and confessed, "You know I am not a water person." Gripping the table like a life raft, I tried to soothe myself with summertime memories of Katie leaping at me from the steps of pools. Katie was deliriously in love with the water and dropped below the surface without hesitation. Taking a bath with her it was I who needed reassurance that we wouldn't drown.

Fawn rocked my right leg. Slosh, slosh. As she moved to wobble my left leg I noticed tension rise around my lungs. The place between my eyes pinched. "I can't breath," I said. My body remembered something. I had recently learned how to make a movie screen out in front of my mind's eye so that my imagination could project images more easily. Immediately, an image of the Titanic came on the screen. I recalled as a child repeatedly singing a haunting song about the Titanic. "Oh it went down, it went down, it went down to the bottom of the sea. Husbands and wives, little children lost their lives. It went down to the bottom of the sea."

But a voice said, "Not the Titanic. It's earlier, an eighteenth-century ship on a transatlantic journey." And a story began to unfold slowly before my eyes. I had left England for America, husbandless with three children, ages two, four, and eight years old. The ship was in a storm, sinking. The children and I were in a cabin and I was screaming, screaming at God, screaming for help, pleading, "Where is God?" No one came. My vocal chords felt raw. My body was completely tense.

Fawn asked, "What is happening with your arms and hands?"

They weren't tense. They were limp and motionless. I cried, "I can't move them." Looking in the screen I saw that something large like an armoire had fallen on me. That was why I was screaming. We were caught and couldn't get out. The ship was going down.

I was living a nightmare. Sobbing, I tried to reassure myself that I was not in fact drowning. Far from relaxed, I was never more grateful to get off a massage table. I got dressed, got in my car and drove down the freeway feeling the need to tell someone what I had been through, that I had died. But, how could I? I was alive and dead at the same time. Who would believe me?

A week or two passed by. Dad came for Christmas. I was still underwater. I couldn't imagine stretching Dad's evangelical Christian mind with the strange story of drowning. It turned out I didn't have to.

On the way home from church he said, "I heard on the radio about a hymn that was written in the 1800s. A woman and her two children were in a ship crossing the Atlantic. The ship sank and her children drowned. When she got to America she sent a telegram to her husband that said, 'Rescued alone.' Later, she and her husband voyaged back to that spot on the Atlantic and the father, Horatio Spafford, wrote this hymn." Dad sang me the chorus.

> *When peace like a river attendeth my way*
> *When sorrows like sea billows roll*
> *Whatever my lot, Thou hast taught me to say*
> *It is well; it is well with my soul.*
> *It is well with my soul. It is well; it is well with my soul.*

Eyes wide open, confounded by the coincidence of my father's words, I blurted out what happened to me. At home we found the hymn in a hymnal and I wondered how Horatio Spafford was able to say, "It is well," after losing his children to the sea? Everything grew heavier in me. I was not at peace. Where was God in tragic death?

The Bible story of Jesus calming the sea surfaced. Reading the gospel of Mark, Chapter 4, it said,

> *A violent squall came up and waves were breaking over the boat, so that it was already filling up. Jesus was in the stern, asleep on a cushion. They woke him and said to him, "Teacher, do you not care that we are perishing?" He woke up, rebuked the wind, and said to the sea, "Quiet! Be still!" The wind ceased and there was a great calm. Then he asked them, "Why are you terrified? Do you not yet have faith?" They were filled with great awe and said to one another, "Who then is this whom even wind and sea obey?"*

Like a frightened disciple, I had no idea about this kind of faith. Tidal waves and vast oceans were the landscapes of my scariest dreams. In one dream I stood on a beach accompanied by an intellectual choreographer, her daughter and my three-year-old, Katie. There were groups of Bosnian women staring out to sea, their dark heads covered, mourning because their children were gone. Suddenly, a wave swept our children under the water. Terrified, I dove into a deep channel only to find the bottom full of bleached, colorless objects, a puppet, a carousel horse, children's toys all whitewashed by time and tide. Nothing was alive. There were no children. At the end of the channel a metal door was shut tight. I realized that Katie must be on the other side.

Returning to the beach, in anguish I told the cool-headed choreographer, "Our children are gone."

"Who is to say that is bad," she said. "Perhaps they are happier."

Shocked by such maternal nonchalance, I wondered how I would tell Stephen that Katie was lost. The powerlessness of motherhood was oceanic in its power and depth.

⚘

Day by day the watery deep surrounded me no matter which way I moved. My friend Trisha Watts sent me her CD, *Deep Waters*, that began with a chant I sang over and over. "Deep waters flowing, calling all to follow, watching, waiting, listening, silence finds a home."

My left eye developed a violent involuntary twitch. Was it fatigue? Sleep brought no relief. When I mentioned the twitch to a stranger on the phone she casually said, "Maybe you've got some grief stuck there."

Every day I lost more energy. I looked everywhere for guidance. Carol Wickersham gave me a prophetic poem called "Swimming Test."

> *Listen when I tell you—*
> *This is the truth of nature:*
> *The level of acceptance is universe*
> *to the level of resistance.*
>
> *7:30 a.m., 13 years old, the first morning*
> *of summer camp. Standing on a splitting dock,*
> *All nipples and goose bumps, anticipating.*
> *The lake's heath rises and falls over the flat, black surface.*

The test is this—dive down
And bring back a stone from the bottom.
Without proof you cannot go on.
You will sit on the shore or wade the edges.

The trick is this—become the stone.
Sink past hearing, past seeing, past telling.
Be hard and cold, so fear will spit you out.
On the way down you must not think about the way up.

This stone is not a diploma, a salary, a prize.
It is a loose front tooth, the first blood on the sheets,
And the last gasp. Go ahead, fight. It will win.
Or embrace it and you may take it by surprise.
Please listen when I tell you—
I know. If I've dived once, I've dived a thousand times.
It is only with a pocketful of stones
That you can glide across the surface.

I was the stone that could not regain the surface. Nothing buoyed me. Seeing the movie, *The Piano*, I sank even deeper when the heroine's piano was thrown into the sea. With her foot caught in the rope, she was pulled overboard by the weighty anchor of her art and life and drowned, eyes pressed wide by the sea.

No longer able to resist the pull of the churning deep, I stopped fighting the water that rose around me. There was nothing to do but let go, even though I resented having one more indescribable experience in a world that would never take this seriously. The sea was in charge. My remaining energy departed. All I could do was sit, cry, and call friends for referrals to therapists.

Finally, I called Phyllis, my clairvoyant friend. After she chastised me for not calling sooner, somehow I got myself to her house. Phyllis closed her eyes to look at my situation and told me, "Cynthia, you are not in your body." She spoke with clarity. Her words were like totems planted alongside my fearful powerful beliefs about death.

She said, "Death is a lie. Spirit creates the body and Spirit doesn't die. You have placed the importance of the body over the importance of the spirit."

It was true. I worked to balance centuries of doctrine that disown the body and split body and soul. Ironically I was out of my body because of my fear of dying in it. I took huge breaths trying to reassure myself. I had an intellectual faith that death was not final and life was continuous, but my cells didn't know it. I heard Jesus say, "Why are you terrified? Do you not yet have faith?"

Phyllis went on, "You feel responsible for the death of the children. But, death comes at the right time."

Having hit my oceanic bottom, her words helped me gently release the idea that I was responsible for the children's death. In doing so, I wondered if this was part of the same fear that drove me to rescue others. Tenderly, I forgave myself for taking my children on a voyage that cost them their lives.

"Well done good and faithful servant," a voice said.

I left feeling relieved to be able to at least function again. But, it was all so weird. Had I been swamped by a past life? Past lives have no place in a Protestant cosmology. As a parting gift, Phyllis handed me a book called *Many Lives, Many Masters* by Brian Weiss. He is a psychologist who recounted encounters with a patient who under hypnotherapy went back to various past lives. Weiss, too, was unsure about what he witnessed, but was moved to write about his patient's remarkable progress. The book both validated what was happening to me and stirred my rebellion against the idea that spirit is superior to the body. Separating spirit from the body diminished life. My questions multiplied. What happens when we die? What about the resurrected body? And how could a minister in the Church admit to having a psychic guide, or that this experience of the resurrection of my body resulted from a past life? To be honest I didn't care. I felt better. When answers were needed, I could find or invent them. I trusted my body and was grateful for the relief in my spirit.

I was still sapped when Phil and I went off to lead a WinterPlay retreat above the Russian River. After the first evening session, Phil suggested I stay and dance. The room was dark, except for silver camp lights pouring through the window. Phil put on a CD and I danced to four pieces of music, stopping briefly between each piece. Physical gestures and images emerged. In the first dance I was underwater but I did not fight: Death. In the second dance my left hand scissored near my twitching eye until I began to thrust with the anger that I had denied. In the third dance I rose from the floor. I was sobbing, suffering a universe of sorrow. During the final dance images from each dance were integrated and to my surprise, I retrieved my lost joy: Acceptance. Joy brought me back to my body.

Amazed, I was no longer tired or heavy. Phil quietly witnessed. I was astonished at how much relief dance brought. How did he know this is what I needed? That movement is soul talk. It's the medicine I needed to move out those things that are buried in me. With renewed energy, I covenanted to regularly "exform" this way, to move what was inside me out with the aid of a witness.

Weird followed weird. Death insisted that I keep learning. On the return trip to the Bay Area, I stopped an hour and a half from home to tell Stephen I was running late.

"Where are you?" he asked.

"In Marin County."

"You have to be here!" he said with intensity.

"I can't. What's going on?"

"I have extreme pain in my right side, a bad fever and can't stand up."

With alarm, I urged, "Go to an emergency room."

"What about Katie?" he asked.

"Call a neighbor to watch her and get someone to take you to emergency. I am coming right home. I'll pick up Katie and come to emergency. Can you do that?"

"Yes."

I got back in my van, trembling. It was happening again. My family needed help and I couldn't reach them.

I crossed one of the Bay bridges. Feeling panic, on the other side

I called Stephen again. This time I only got the answering machine. Trying to remain calm, I looked at my watch. It was 5:15 p.m. Hands on the wheel, I remembered Christ and my angel. I prayed, "Stephen might die. I know I can only do what I can do. Please go to Stephen. Let me know you are with him. I am willing for whatever happens to happen." As I spoke these words my chest filled with an unusual calm as if an angel were sitting in the center of my chest, an angel who was also with Stephen. The rest of the drive home was peaceful. Whenever I started to worry, I checked the feeling in my chest. It was calm.

At home I found Katie at our neighbor's house. As I grabbed her hand to go to the hospital my neighbor said, "I just got a call that Stephen is coming home." Ten minutes later Stephen was in our living room.

"What happened?" I asked.

"I don't know. I was sitting in the emergency room, full of fever and pain and then around 5:20, the fever broke and the pain went away so they sent me home. "

I stared at him in disbelief. "Stephen, at 5:15 p.m. I prayed to Christ and my angel to be with you."

The following morning I had an appointment with Flora Wuellner, my spiritual director. So much was happening. I told her about the drowning, the angel in my chest, and the dances that brought me relief on the weekend. Thank God for spiritual directors who don't question these things, but understand that each of us interacts with a world of mystery, helping us navigate and grow our connection to the Divine.

After Flora gave me her unconditional attention, she pulled Walt Whitman's *Leaves of Grass* from her shelf. Flipping through it she came to his poem "Assurances." She handed it to me and I read,

> *I do not doubt that the passionately-wept deaths*
> *of young men are provided for, and that the deaths*

of young women and the deaths of little children are
provided for.

(Did you think Life was so well provided for, and
Death, the purport of all Life is not well provided
for?)

I do not doubt that wrecks at sea, no matter what
the horrors of them, no matter whose wife, child,
husband, father, lover has gone down, are provided
for, to the minutest points.

I do not doubt that whatever can possibly happen
anywhere at anytime, is provided for in the inher-
ences of things.

I do not think Life provides for all and for Time
and Space, but I believe Heavenly Death provides
for all.

Walt Whitman believed in life beyond death. Having been a chaplain to hundreds of dying soldiers and as one who was intimate with the eastern seaboard's tragic and stormy seas, he saw the sea as the baptistry for the inevitable.

Flora spoke softly to me. She proposed that we pray for all those who drowned during the sinking of the ship. She reminded me that Jesus functioned well in storms. Following her lead, I closed my eyes. Indeed, I saw that Jesus was not afraid. He who walked on water was not subject to it. Although I was fully grown, he took me in his arms. I trusted him as we slowly submerged, noticing that I could still breathe as we journeyed underwater to the ship. Then I saw what I could not see when I was afraid. Christ had always been with me and my children in the tiny cabin. As the children departed, he dried them off. Then I, too, went peacefully.

This was when I learned the meaning of Horatio Spafford's hymn. Rescued from the depths, a resurrected body, I knew that it was well with my soul. Humbled and yes, even "saved," I leaned heavily on the faithful arms of people like Phyllis, Horatio Spafford, Walt Whitman, Flora Wuellner and mystics like Isaiah whose words became more than poetry, more than wishful thinking when he said, "Thy dead shall live, my body shall rise, O dwellers in the dust, awake and sing for joy."

No wonder I hated to swim. That didn't change after all this praying. When Julie Caffey heard my story of drowning she said she had helped other water phobic people and offered me swimming lessons. I knew that transforming bodily fear required giving one's muscles new memories. Could I move drowning out of my body memory?

At the San Francisco YMCA, Julie gave me goggles and we dunked beneath the surface, joking, gesturing, and playing tea party like kids. But when she asked me to put my head under and blow out my nose, my lungs demanded breath. I worked to iron out the panic reflex, exhaling slowly, watching bubbles race up to the surface.

As I improved she gave me my next step, "Now open your mouth and swallow water. Drowning is part of swimming."

I knew it!

She took this even further during lesson two. I had to float face down with eyes shut. Each time I pushed off from the edge and hung suspended in stillness, gravity pulled me down and I flailed. Float. Flail. Float. Flail. Julie held me as I exhaled and descended, but the panic intensified. I came up sputtering.

As a last resort, I focused on Christ holding me. Pushing off from the edge, I glided, floated, exhaled bubbles and sank. When I surfaced Julie's eyes were soft. She said, "That is the first time you let your body sink that far down."

"I am supposed to sink?" I asked confused.

She nodded yes. One last time, I let Christ hold me as I glided, floated, and exhaled. I didn't fight or control. I sank. When I came up, I looked at Julie and wept. Wasn't this a baptism?

Nothing in my rational, feminist, twentieth century education clued me in that a real baptism could proceed from a past life drowning on a ship or that trust in God through death itself would come at a YMCA pool. Liturgy is rehearsal. It is rarely the real deal. Plus this was my third baptism. The official one happened in my infancy at a Methodist church. An innocuous splash of water on my head that reinforced how innocent and sweet I looked, was a mere pre-initiation setting the stage for the big waves to come.

A second baptism happened onstage at the Purdue Hall of Music in front of 5,000 Presbyterian women. Phil, Judith and I, improvising baptism as a dance, were dressed in white gowns. With music playing, we waded into a stage-crafted baptistry. The audience didn't expect real water and I didn't expect the experience of adult immersion. Leaning back in Judith's arms, the waters came over me. I came up gasping, as surprised as everyone else by the physicality of surrender. Judith turned me toward the 5,000 women and the theater was transformed. I was baptized as a dancer before a sea of women.

Should I be surprised? The prayer of my life was to acquaint myself with the dance of life. Had I been forewarned that this prayer always includes intimacy with its opposite, the dance of death, I would have been more afraid.

Learning lessons of life and death, I understood that for those who remain open to experience, prayers are answered in our body, that Christ's love is profoundly physical, that the Bible is not just an old tale of boring supernatural adventures. It's a portal to a multidimensional world where things that don't make sense in our world can be recognized and healed. And that each of us can enter a dreamtime where Jesus or some other figure leads us to the power that transcends death and powerlessness if only we have been given the keys to our kinesthetic imagination and used them to unlock the mysteries of faith.

> *Then Jesus made his disciples get into the boat and precede him to the other side toward Bethsaida, while he dismissed the crowd. And when he had taken leave of them, he went off to the mountain to pray. When it was evening, the boat was far out on the sea and he was alone on shore. Then he saw that they were tossed about while rowing, for the wind was against them. About the fourth watch of the night he came towards them walking on the sea, they thought it was a ghost and cried out. They had all seen him and were terrified. But at once he spoke with them, "Take courage, it is I, do not be afraid!" He got into the boat with them and the wind died down.*

> *They were completely astounded. They had not under-*
> *stood the incident of the loaves. On the contrary, their*
> *hearts were hardened.*   —MARK 6: 45-52, RSV

Salvation means what it means. The soul is saved from final death. But, like the disciples I am sorely tempted to see, but not believe. To progress in mystical life, one has to both honor and suspend intellect, opening the heart to uncomfortable words of faith that sound as exclusive as they are life saving. I walked a bridge between imaginal and real and found that life embraced both.

Heart, be not hardened anymore.

Just days after the mythic drowning, Stephen invited his ailing father, Joe, to live with us. I was hardly prepared to take in an invalid. After a day of huffing around, I settled down, rearranged the house, moved our bed into the den, bought Joe a bed, and purchased shoes that he could slip into without help. He was seventy-eight, had a catheter and could barely bathe or walk. The doctor's advice was, "Try to keep him comfortable."

Meanwhile, three-year-old Katie woke up one morning complaining that her bottom was sore. Taking her to the doctor's office, our active, happy toddler crawled around on the exam room floor as we awaited urine test results. When the doctor squeezed into the room, a little red light flashed in her eyes as she said officiously, "The sugar in Katie's urine indicates she could have diabetes. Our machine may not be working right, but we need to admit her for further tests just to be safe."

Admit? I wanted to shake the doctor. My body puffed up and shot electrical currents. Do other mothers go wacko in medical offices? As I expanded in fear, Stephen contracted. Instead of leaving with ointment or pills, we headed for the pediatric wing. Fighting back fiery tears, I took a stab at turning this into a "special-field-trip-in-the-hospital" for Katie. Who was I kidding?

"Why is Mommy crying? "Katie asked Stephen in front of the elevator.

I dashed into the gift shop, tears erupting through the maternal place in my psyche.

"Catastrophic Thinker! Catastrophic Thinker!" a voice accused.

"I don't do out of control!" I shouted back in defense.

Oceanic fear thundered toward me as I careened toward a hospital volunteer in a blue apron behind the counter. With my eyes bugging out and my emotional clothes hanging somewhere around my knees, I sputtered, "They're admitting my daughter for diabetes!"

She grabbed my hand without missing a beat, "I know. It never goes away, not even when they get older. My daughter is thirty and it feels just the same." Then she handed me a stuffed purple Barney dinosaur and said, "Here, give this to your daughter." I was not alone. A blue-dress lady with a purple dinosaur saved me. I returned to Katie and Stephen saying to myself, "I can do this."

Room 354 had one empty bed. The other belonged to Christi, a seven-year-old, permanent resident who was so lonely that she immediately crawled into our laps and then in bed with Katie, I ran to the phone to call everyone I knew to pray for us.

Every couple of hours a nurse attempted to draw Katie's blood, fishing unsuccessfully for a vein until Katie screamed, "No more pokey! No more pokey!" Waiting for results from the blood tests, time tripped over itself, stopping for eternity and then thrusting forward until night came.

Stephen couldn't watch Katie be poked one more time. Exhausted, he went home at 8:00 p.m. For the last time the nurses put her on an exam table to take her blood. Katie panted, screamed, and looked at me in disbelief as I held her little face. Unfortunately she hadn't learned how to say, "Mother, you idiot! Make them stop." I let them take her blood.

At 9:00 p.m. a doctor said all the tests were negative. We could go home. Another child also tested false positive for diabetes that day. They were going to check their machine. Was I grateful? Hell no. I was angry. If this was part of the dance of motherhood, God help us all.

Scott Galuteria was in Wing It! This dark-haired Hawaiian boy-king was a tropical flower who opened easily to others. Before being diagnosed as HIV positive he served as a flight attendant who could break into King of Siam impersonations for air travelers, ordering everyone around. Scott also danced hula and sang with the Gay Men's Chorus.

Scott's hospitalizations increased as his body weight and strength decreased. Tuesday, February 15, 1994, I went to see him in the hospital, expecting to stay an hour or two. Scott's mom, his brother Brickwood, his close friend Kevin, and partner Frank had been there for days, planning who would be there and how Scott's death would transpire. The entrance of Wing It! was unplanned. Because we were improvising we could clearly see that the end was near. When Scott's immediate family left to shower and rest, I questioned if they should go.

Scott, full of pneumonia, sounded like he was drowning. Fresh from my watery memories, like Lazarus looking back into the tomb, I felt strangely assured that all would be well.

When Scott left his body. I felt the shift. He was still breathing, but the room was different. I got light-headed like I did in the drowning. Ungroundedness swept through me and holding Scott's hand made me nauseous. I recognized these sensations as the feeling of leaving the body. I was amazed at my ability to feel the sensations of Scott's body in my own.

Frank, Scott's lover, came in and sat next to Scott. With eyes closed, Frank began sobbing. His hand went to his heart as a torrent broke forth. I've never seen that much liquid leave a face. Phil held his shoulder. Later Frank said that Scott had entered his heart, consoling and dancing with him.

I kept changing the cloth on Scott's forehead, wondering where his family and friends were. Dusk fell outside the hospital window. Finally, Scott's mother returned and a song by Karl Harrington came to me.

> *There's a song in the air.*
> *There's a star in the sky.*
> *There's a mother's deep prayer*

and a baby's low cry.
And a star reigns from heaven
and the beautiful sing
For a manger in Bethlehem cradles a King.

It was the nativity in reverse. Instead of being born in a cradle, this King departed from one. Mother and child labored with AIDS in manger 1008, tenth floor, St. Francis Hospital—"the resort," Frank and Scott called it. Inside those four pale walls exotic gifts were laid at his feet: leis, lavender oil for anointing, dim sum, croissants, and macadamia nuts. Instead of angel song, strains from Roger's and Hammerstein's *The King and I* floated through the space.

Shall we dance? Shall we then say good night but
mean good-bye?
Or perchance when the last little star has left the sky
Shall we still be together with our arms around each
other?
And shall you be my new romance?
With the clear understanding that this kind of thing
can happen
Shall we dance? Shall we dance? Shall we dance?

At 9:30 p.m., Brickwood beckoned his mother into the room. Joining hands we returned to a hymn that we had sung at morning and noontime.

He touched me, He touched me,
and oh what joy that floods my soul.
Something happened and now I know
He touched me, and made me whole.

I squeezed Phil's hand and watched Scott's exhale grow longer than his inhale. Then, inevitably and unthinkably, Scott's breath halted on the end of the verse. His mom wept, her son in her arms, a pieta in death's manger.

That semester as I taught my annual spring class at Pacific School of Religion, I was not prepared when the new seminary president, the first woman to fill that position and the only president willing to dance, abruptly laid off of six staff, including the Dean of Students and Vice President of Finance. Students hung the campus with black crepe paper. A drum droned in front of her office. Sidewalks were chalked with accusations. Letters of explanation and blame stuffed the mailboxes. Anxiety passed from body to body, faculty to faculty, student to student. Spiritual beasties promenaded the open square.

Being an adjunct faculty, I had no direct communication with faculty or staff. Struggling to sort through garbage heaps of gossip, I eventually decided to take my adjunct role seriously. Unable to address the wounds directly, I stuck with chasing the dance and did not mention the drama outside. I watched as dance led us through the relational land mines that we brought into the room. Dance healed the wounded community faster than discussion. It released tension and created energy when there was none. Each week we danced back to the arms of grace as best as we could, consistently surprised when we walked away better off for it. Dance retrieved our hope and carried more than a real possibility of resurrecting the body of the community.

If hard things come in threes I was beyond my limit. Easter week my close friend Susan called from Los Angeles to say, "I have a lump in my breast, and I am going to have a biopsy." Two days later she said, "It's malignant."

Susan and I had traveled similar bumpy roads through seminary and ministry. I was also there when Susan's dad died and her mom committed suicide. Susan was there when Stephen had his accident and when Katie went to the hospital. We shared similar infertility and adoption journeys. To top it off Susan and I looked similar. When she went to my hair stylist, the hairdresser asked if she had a sister. Susan said, "Yes."

I flew to L.A. to see her. As always, Susan showed me her wounds. She still had to undergo a double mastectomy, reconstructive surgery and radiation.

I asked, "When should I come back?"

"Don't come." She answered.

"Don't come?" For the first time she drew a thick line around her to create a privacy that didn't include me.

On the day of her mastectomy I did the only thing I could. I took care of myself. I rested, bathed, ate, drew, read and prayed for Susan by caring for my own body. I didn't go to her. I went to myself. That was all I could do. That and dance my fear in all of its terrible majesty during Wing It! practices.

W. H. Auden wrote, "Dance, dance the figure is easy. The tune is catching and will not stop; Dance till the stars come down from the rafters. Dance, dance, dance, till you drop." I'd survived the drowning episode, Scott's death, P.S.R.'s chaos, Katie's day in the hospital, Joe's deterioration, Susan's breast cancer. I thought, O.K., that's it, right? Instead, whoever was in charge of my doctorate in death slapped me with roadwork.

Three days in a row I watched animals die while I was driving. A cat ran onto the on-ramp ahead of me and was hit. The next day a second cat splintered under a wheel. On day three all I saw was a woman kneel on the median strip, crumpled over the body of a dead animal. I pulled over and wept.

An inner voice demanded, "Cynthia, now let go of meaning. Just dance." The biggest thing I had to let go of were my notions of a reasonable God. That God was dying, too.

When Katie got chicken pox I laughed hysterically. Bring on the childhood diseases! Come on, I could take it. Instead, Joe turned blue. Five paramedics in giant yellow gaiters stomped into our ten-by-ten foot bedroom. We needed a movie set for this much action. They carried Joe off on a stretcher for the first of several emergency trips to the hospital. Our bungalow became a medical center as nurses bathed Joe in the only bathroom, prepared food in our kitchen, and sat with him in our bedroom. He was depressed, bossy, and told sleazy jokes. Grabbing at the fleeting corners of my privacy, I watched it slip away just when I needed it most.

On the autumn equinox, September 21st, death knocked at our door. I could smell it. Even with the front door wide open and six living bodies in the house, it smelled stale. My heart hung open too. Joe was quieter. His needs were immediate: ice chips, a pillow, buttermilk, a popsicle, having his diaper changed (still hard to say that), help to turn on his side, cream for his raw leg. There was less TV. The stillness intensified. I looked in at him rubbing his arm as though it were the most important work in the world, each action, and a final benediction.

As his arms and lungs filled with fluid his cough scared me. He was drowning. Morphine came as an angel along with aides, social workers, and equipment deliverers. I couldn't make small talk anymore. When each helper left I felt both abandoned and relieved. Learning to behave with propriety all the time, make sure we were dressed and acting kosher, I was way past smiling. I craved predictability. If someone didn't show up or changed their schedule, I fumed. Time had turned into a twisty river, and I was at the whim of its current.

Stephen was on alert. Having lost his Mom to cancer at age twelve, he'd become the chaplain to many dying people, offering his presence as one who had met and lived with death his whole life.

On September 22, 1994, Joe celebrated his seventy-ninth birthday. His youngest son, Mark, phoned from Delphi, Greece. His middle son, Rich, and his wife came bearing Joe's last request, a cherry cake with orange frosting and pineapple pieces, one of Joe's notorious food concoctions.

That night at four a.m. I lay down. Could I do the death dance with Joe? All the threads of body connection with him that were once invisible now felt pulled taut. In the morning I knew I had to leave. Katie and I kissed Joe's elbow and forehead and said good-bye. Flying to my niece's first birthday in L.A., Katie asked why I was crying. I told her, "I think Grandpa Joe will die today."

"Mommy," said Katie, "it's just like an apple seed. You put it in the ground, up it comes a tree, then down and up, again and again."

I called Stephen every three hours.

At 2 a.m. on Sunday the phone rang and Stephen said, "He's dead."

Back home I entered the bedroom and sat on the stool where Stephen had kept watch. Katie crawled on Joe's empty bed, then fetched me a doll and took our dog out to the front porch. Joe's shoes were still under the bed. The oxygen tank was finally silent but the smell remained.

Joe wanted cremation. At the mortuary a cardboard box with packing tape and a plastic bag stuck out from the bottom shelf. It cost thirty dollars. The next box up cost $400.00. We chose the cardboard even though it felt cheap. Joe wouldn't burn $400.00.

My legs ached. It was phenomenal work to lose a parent. Just sitting made me groan. Monday, Tuesday, and Wednesday I began to clean, tell the story, and decide things. I piled old clothes in our truck, except a few nice sweaters. The hospital bed was taken. The oxygen tank was taken. Two flower arrangements arrived. My friend Carol came to help me wash Joe's walls. I left some things where they were: the last book he read, *The River's End*, his wedding picture, a collage of his family, *The Carleton Voice* (his alumni magazine), two birthday cards, a hymnal, and a photo of him standing and smiling a year ago.

Joe was dead.

I think I got the diploma for my doctorate in death shortly after that.

Death scoured me. Words became simpler. Silence was richer. The only aftershock was that my hair turned grey. I wasn't depressed, cut down, or ill at ease. Sharing my tales of death with an audience of AIDS caregivers, I declared that if I hadn't grieved so wholeheartedly, singing, laughing, crying, and dancing in community, I'd be grieving still. They gave me a standing ovation. Acquainted with constant death, they'd discovered the same thing.

❀

Stephen's childhood home, Joe's house, sold in a month to a guy who tore it down. We put our house on the market, too. With InterPlay centered fifty miles away in Oakland, Joe's pension gone, and Katie about to start kindergarten, commuting wasn't a luxury I could afford.

Putting a "For Sale" sign on the lawn, I contemplated all that had happened in our house. Poppy, our little fox-faced dog, found us at church already house-trained and patient as a monk. Her only fault was shedding mountains of her white undercoat of fur on every sur-face of our furniture. Katie was born and the next thing we knew she was opening Christmas presents on the living room floor and smear-ing garden tomatoes all over her face. In our remodeled kitchen Stephen and I let go of the church and learned to dream again. Stephen enrolled in an actor's conservatory and I turned the garage into an office to make money at the business of art.

465 Flagg was not just a house.

> *Home is verb*
> *unstoppable longing*
> *thrown alongside inhospitable worlds,*
> *a private kitchen counter-revolution*
> *safeguarding sounds of the child*
> *among strains of snatched peace.*
> *where eyes pray on small things*
> *linoleum, pansy-rooted soil, shelf*
> *paper, doily spotted family photo,*
> *gentle weapons*
> *wielded against life's violent winds.*
>
> *Shelter isn't made by code or doctrine.*
> *It's honed by faith and instinct*
> *using hope's unturned stone,*
> *the one that chants, "You're home!"*
> *That I wept here without solace*

made love, rearranged each molecule,
makes leaving it another death.
And in releasing this rough-hewn Eden
exposes the over-collected inner rummage
ever dancing toward decay.

Thank God the house didn't sell. Months went by. Joe must have been looking out for us. Only when I was ready did Lisa Lopez-Williams, an Irish-Mexican Catholic, give me a small plastic statue of Joseph holding baby Jesus and the instructions, "Bury him upside down in your backyard. It will help your house sell." But, the statue was so cute I put him on the fireplace mantle. When a Mexican family looked at the house they seemed interested, but another month passed with no solid offers. Desperately, I took Saint Joseph off the mantle, went to the backyard, and as unceremoniously as a post digger, planted the Holy Father's head straight down in the dirt. I brushed the dirt off my hands, went inside, lit a candle, and prayed to both Saint Joseph and Joe Henry to let the house sell. Three days later the Mexican family made an offer and bought the house.

We found a mint green house on the island of Alameda, a secret Midwest-style town in the heart of the bustling Bay Area. I fell in love with its large leafy trees, Ole's Waffle Shop, Tucker's Ice Cream, and the Park Street Ballet. The only way to get on the island was by drawbridge. Alamedans weren't keen on growth and I was pretty sick of it myself. At the Chamber of Commerce, the city manager said, "Alameda is a friendly place, but it takes a few generations to live here."

Moving day, I dug up the plastic Joseph, washed the detritus off of him, stuck him on the dashboard, and drove north in a U-Haul full of domestic objects. As I maneuvered it into the new drive, Katie looked up at me from the sidewalk stunned. "You driving the truck, Mommy?" I smiled down at her. It was Mother's day and I was happy. It was a new beginning. There were no crossed wires out of the front window and no church job. Stephen and I were both twenty minutes from work. Katie's kindergarten was a block away, where the PTA still made field trips, computers, and assemblies a reality. A voice inside urged,

Snatch up your dangling roots
run quick to new dirt,
make your garden again
illuminate new mantles,
kindly place chair, photo,
bedspread, clock, and plate.
Let the Goddess of Hearth
confirm this home as
the shape of your heart.

To celebrate turning forty, I wanted to go white water rafting. Mother Lode Rafting Company offered a two-day river trip. I invited my friends to join me on Memorial Day weekend as I joked about preparing to undo my bad water karma. Many laughed. Some surprisingly signed up.

May 26th sixteen of us gathered at the river. Heavy winter floods had made the river run faster and higher than it had in years. "No problem," said the owner of Mother Lode. I was happy to be surrounded by friends who loved water: artists, spirit folk, fun lovers, nuns, body workers, corporate exiles, teachers, Latin translators, counselors, Buddhists, and philosophers. Many loved to swim, except Jo, a fifty-year-old Minnesotan with a respiratory disorder. She confessed she hadn't told her mother where she was going. Margie Brown wasn't too stable on land either. An effortlessly wacky biblical storyteller-clown with cerebral palsy, she could never pass up a good party. Who was I to stop her? That night we pitched our tents next to the snow cold river as it drummed against our psyches, blotting out all extraneous thought.

May 27th at 10:30 a.m., the Mother Lode staff gathered us and two other groups for an orientation—or was it "The Warning?" That's when the man in charge admitted that this was not just another day on the river. The current was moving faster than normal. He gave us a strict list of dos and don'ts. Avoid deadly "strainers," submerged trees that drag you under. Due to the danger of hypothermia, avoid getting in the water. If the raft hits a rock, get to the "high side of the raft," the side that the river tries to flip. If thrown out, point the feet downstream like a corpse and float. None of this was on the four-color brochure.

As he demonstrated the mechanics of getting dragged back in the boat I watched my friends grow slightly more hysterical. We were going to get wet. I gripped the earth and signed the paper releasing Mother Lode from responsibility for my death.

We poured our fleshy bodies into fish skin wet suits and donned orange life jackets. Topped with a wool sweater, socks, and water sandals from Payless Drug Store I was relieved that my swimming teacher, Julie, was in my boat. So was Stephen.

Dr. Margie spoke to the lead guide about her balance problems while the rest of us got oars. By no logic whatsoever we grouped ourselves. Margie was led to a boatload of strangers while I grabbed Leslie the kayaker and Roxanne the canoer. Catching Margie's eye, I could see her unhappiness so I latched onto her and said, "Come with us."

A guide in her twenties with long hair, a ball cap, and sweet eyes took our boat. When the Mother Lode manager, Joe, checked on our group, I reminded him of Margie's difficulty. He asked our guide, "Can you handle this?"

I knew it was not a question you ask a competent guide. Worse, our guide's hesitation lasted several endless seconds, careening down my intuitive gut like boulders down a well. Oh, Fateful Premonition. Why did he ask that?

Finally she said, "I think I can handle it."

I looked over at Joe and back at the guide, praying to find confidence. Considering that I might be getting in another sinking boat, I demanded, "I want a hundred percent on this."

"You can handle this?" he asked the guide again.

"Yes," she said with a seventy-five percent nod. As we got in the raft, uncertainty settled in with us.

Before moving to the center of the river, those of us who were water-shy practiced falling out of the boat. Taking a deep breath, we fell in, got wet, shivered, and got hauled back in. Having no intention of falling out in white water, I grounded myself and made the boat heavy with my will.

With the morning sun rising in the sky, our six little rafts took for-mation and swept into the bulging current. All of a sudden our guide quickly taught us commands like Stroke! Bail! Oars left back! Right forward! Maneuvering the yellow boat through coursing waves, we cued off of Julie whose strength set our pace. It was no picnic. We were a nervous boatload of professional communicators and bossy InterPlayers who demanded that our guide speak clear enough to cue us so we could understand her, frantic to follow our leader.

I pretended like I had rafted for years. A good faker, I approached each mountain of liquid turbulence and improvised. I was in the moment. Oars flew. Bodies plunged. Margie held tight. Water swamped us. Stephen bailed. I stroked. Hitting a white thunderous roar, Julie catapulted. Roxanne followed. I clamped Roxanne's legs and pulled her back in the boat. Julie floated alongside, tensely smil-ing and saying "I'm O.K." Her feet were pointed down stream. In seconds we pulled her two hundred pounds back in the raft.

We already had a story to tell. We laughed. We groaned. Intensity was a fast teacher. Each time the river sucked us in and spit us out, we met it, stroking, bailing, and sinking deeper into our yellow dingy. That is until an unexpected set of rapids appeared. Undulating and out of control, we fell into a watery hole, spun, and water filled the boat.

When the river finally spat us out, our guide exclaimed, "We surfed!" making near death sound like a party. Thank goodness it was time for lunch. The hospitality of the guides who prepared the meal relaxed everyone. I ate everything in sight, glad to be alive.

The afternoon proceeded in a similar way until we reached the reservoir. Rafters began jumping into the water on purpose, their black-slickered bodies floating free in the chilly current. With the end in sight, I fearlessly fantasized about an endless journey down-river, glad there was another day of rafting.

For the evening entertainment we watched pictures taken of us battling the rapids. In one photo all you could see was our guide. The rest of us had disappeared behind a wall of water. The next round of photos were of past river doozies: people flying, springing, and crashing in and out of rafts. Over and over a river rock called "Trouble Maker" caught our attention. We had yet to encounter it.

That night, on the eve of turning forty, I dreamt that my mother died. It seemed a factual event that stirred little emotion. I was growing up.

On Sunday morning, May 28th, my birthday, my usually gregarious friends spoke quietly of last words, wills, regrets, and desires. Jo resolved not to raft that day. After all, she couldn't swim. I, too, had a premonition that something was going to happen.

The bus was heaped with rafts like a Dr. Seuss top hat. Graveling uphill in low, low, low gear toward Sutter's Creek, its precarious torque and sway agitated our fears. On the other side of the ridge we looked down on a mania of yellow, orange, and blue rafts advertising their company insignias. Around them a cloud of human electricity buzzed as hundreds of white water novices from Apple Computer, Pacific Telephone, the Navy Cadets, and us, a cast of Spiritual Fools, all prepared to let loose of our moorings.

Teaming up with the same guides, our group took the same spots like church members lashed superstitiously to a pew. At least that was secure. I noticed Jo get in a raft in spite of her fears as I issued birthday hats to everyone to wear for the pictures to be taken at Trouble Maker. Our young, bill-capped guide warned us that the day's rapids would begin immediately. There was to be no warm up.

Courageously, we "put in," like a line of little ducklings struggling against a mean current. The lead raft went first. We were fourth or fifth in the line. I psychically transformed my legs into old tree roots reaching through gallons of turbulent liquid. Stroke, stroke, left side, right side, back, back. We dug into the resistant river, oars arguing impossibly with the raucous current. Remember to breathe, I told myself.

Hitting the center of the river, intense explosions of cresting water beat down on us. Were these rapids a class three or four? Whatever. We were out of our class! Stephen bailed; Margie battened herself down in the bottom of the boat. We spun, surfed, filled, and bailed. Were we supposed to be this out of control? During a brief stretch of smooth, fast water, Stephen and Julie used two buckets to get rid of the water. It wasn't enough. We were too heavy to even get to the bank where other rafts were emptying out.

I tried to stroke as more water poured in. We'll be OK, I thought, if we can just get to the bank. Instead, our guide drove us toward some submerged trees. We reached out for branches, skin ripping from our hands.

Careening sideways, headed for a thick web of alders, I yelled, "We're going to hit the trees!" As we plowed into them, the river pushed us up against them.

Someone yelled, "Get to the high side!" and we threw our weight against the violent water beating and bouncing us into the clot of trees. Looking into each other's eyes, we sensed the danger we were in. Our stunned guide was silent. Literally in over her head with us, the river poured over our limbs. Leslie and I held Margie inside the boat. Turning blue, rattling with cold, we held onto each other and made one attempt to push ourselves toward the bank which only wedged us deeper.

Being a boat full of amusement queens, we managed to take a picture of ourselves with a throwaway water camera. I joked and apologized to everyone for dragging them through my old drowning karma. Someone quipped that we all had our own reasons for getting in the boat.

"Well, who has the bad tree karma?" I asked.

Roxanne, sheepish, admitted, "Me! But that's another story."

A raft went by. We shouted to them as if anyone could miss us. Gradually fifteen rafts and professional guides huddled on the bank just down river. People scaled a cliff to survey our situation, including friends intent on keeping us in their sights. There was Fawn on whose Trager table I had remembered drowning, Terri who swam with dolphins, Chinh, the former Vietnamese boat person, and Phil whose favorite place was in the shower. Jo wouldn't watch. She just prayed.

Somehow, seven he-men thrust themselves from the shore, pitting sheer muscle against the current as they crossed to the stand of alders. We watched as two guys walked through the forbidden trees, stretching an orange rope toward us. They yelled, "We're going to walk you down to the other boat." By then, Mother Lode Joe's boat was fastened to the alders, too.

The guides took Margie first. It was a good thing. If Jesus had asked Margie to walk on water, she would've done it. She had crazy faith. Although cerebral palsy usually caused Margie to fall down, she had no problem walking through the treetops.

With the guides' help the rest of us formed one line. Holding onto each other and the bright orange rope, our legs groped for something to land on as the hostile river twisted and buckled our feet. Julie flailed, grabbed my back and screamed, "Wait!" as she tried to right herself. The woman who had taught me to drown lost her calm.

Many terrified prayers carried us to the rafts where the river guides muscled up twelve Herculean strokes and landed us back on the shore. Meanwhile Joe was still mid-river, retrieving our empty raft. We watched as he threw our oars into the current, manually pulling the oarless boat through the thicket until it swept downstream with him in it. Catching a rope flung by a guide, he and the raft were hauled in.

The steep, crowded bank gave us no option but to get back in our raft. We were frozen, wild-eyed, and delirious from adrenalin. Our young guide looked undone. Four of our seven oars were in a boat downriver. In spite of just having lost our minds to cold and fear, when someone instructed, "Go get 'em," we idiotically shoved off like amputees racing down a flight a stairs.

Instantly, the current engulfed us again and we struggled to get to the side. As our guide yelled commands, we grabbed at trees. Then she jumped into the river as if to personally secure the raft to the bank with her body. But, the water was deep and swimming was impossible. Talk about going overboard. I grabbed her and dragged her back in.

I don't know how we stopped or got our oars. We just did. Trembling and angry, we yelled at the other boats, "We have to stop! We need rest. We need food." Joe brought snacks and reassurance. I wanted a different guide and new raft mates. I wanted to redistribute the trauma that had collected in our boat. But, a vocal guide emphasized that we should stay together. I didn't have enough will left to assert myself.

Trouble Maker was ahead. We drank tea, ate nuts, and shook. While dismissing my intuition to separate our party, I demanded a change. Stephen would take my position at the front where he could apply his strength and I would bail.

Fifteen minutes later, back in the river, we reminded each other to breathe and screamed out our terror like warriors. To survive Trouble Maker, I had to banish my fear of drowning. I put my hands firmly on the oars, faced downriver, gathered up all my old water anxiety into an intense energy ball, and sent it out to the Pacific Ocean. I exploded my fear like the last fireworks on the Fourth of July. Ka-Bluey!

Within the hour, the inevitable happened. Approaching Trouble Maker, our guide aimed right over the top of it and into the sucking vacuum. White water swallowed us like a hungry lion. For an eternity of seconds we submerged. Bodies swam around in the bottom of the raft. There was nothing to grab onto. Miraculously, no one flew out. Just as abruptly, the river spit us out.

I bailed as the river widened and grew quiet. No one spoke. Approaching the bank for a final lunch our guide fell overboard one last time. Margie, Leslie, Stephen, Roxanne, Julie, and I climbed over the yellow rubber ledge; our feet touched the earth and out tears spilled. We lay down, squatted, and held each other.

Regaining our composure we ate lunch. Guides whispered phrases like "most dangerous," and "wondered how to do a rescue like that." They left us alone. We had one more leg to go.

Getting back in the boat for the last time, we knew we were survivors. In my case I not only survived my birthday, I transcended my fear of drowning. We did what camp counselors do, we sang songs. Our guide taught us one of her favorites. "A river is flowing, flowing and going down to the sea. Mother carry me, your child I will always be. Mother carry me, your child I will always be." We sang right along with her.

In the following months, like survivors of any natural disaster, we talked incessantly, reliving and recounting the morning of May 28th to anyone who would listen. I had discovered a great way for friends either to remember or blot out your birthday. Terrify them.

5 | Initiations

The transformations that await us cost everything in the way of courage and sacrifice. Let no one be deluded that knowledge of the path can substitute for putting one foot in front of the other. Centering is a severe and thrilling discipline, often acutely unpleasant. In my own efforts, I become weak, discouraged, exhausted, angry, frustrated, unhappy and confused. But someone within me is resolute, and I try again. Within us lies a merciful being who helps us to our feet however many times we fall.
—MARY RICHARDS, *CENTERING*

IN THE OAKLAND HILLS THERE IS A LABYRINTH hidden at the bottom of a quarry. The spiral sits by a bog where frogs alternately croak and listen. New Years Day, Carol and I decided to pay it a visit. Looking down on the circuitous path, two women whose feet were happy to dangle over the edge of mystery, it was a beautiful sight.

Down in the quarry, we sat quietly for a while. Then Carol entered the labyrinth. The frogs sang to her. Reaching the center she picked up a book that was balanced on the center rock, a brand new artist's sketchbook. Carol had a degree in art but very little time for it as a pastor and a mom. She flipped through empty drawing pages and decided to take it. Happy New Year.

It was my turn. I told Carol, "This year I want less drama," and put my foot to the muddy path. At a stretch of oozing mud, to avoid getting all messed up like usual, I stepped on the rocks, teetered, wobbled, my arms jerking, grasping for invisible handles in the air. I twisted my ankle, but at least I was clean. The frogs were silent.

Was there something in the center for me, too? I peered down at

123

the little rock altar built up by previous walkers. There were sticks and flowers, coins, burnt things, small scrolled messages, and a lapel button. Bending over, I picked it up. Written in black letters on a pink background were these words, "Touch me. Touch me. I love it when you violate my space."

I howled. Was it a holy kick-in-the butt joke or a prophecy? I'd just devoted ten years to acknowledging I'd been violated and dedicated myself to learn ways to protect my space. I had given up on church in order to learn healthy protection. Weren't violation and abuse the enemy?

Perhaps I had learned my lessons and was being given new ones. The Universe wants me to dance with EVERYTHING! It wasn't going to let me stand on one belief or leg forever. A wise teacher said, "What you resist persists." The button reminded me that if I feared violation, I would continuously experience it. Resistance to suffering creates suffering.

"Touch me, Touch me. I love it when you violate my space," said Spirit with its maddening wisdom. I stuck the button on my chest. I picked up a long stick for balance as I exited the labyrinth. The stick hit bedrock. The mud was less than an inch thick. My precarious rock hopping was all to avoid an inch of mud. Was this true of life's dramas too?

I took off my shoes, rolled up my pants and stepped into the gooey sludge. Brown muck curled around my stringy toes. A voice said, "No mess is as deep as you think. Move sensually through all you resist."

Five years had passed since leaving the pastorate. I still felt like a fugitive from an institutional crime. The church was encoded in my DNA, but I didn't trust myself there. Apparently resisting it was futile, so I started driving fifty miles to Peace Lutheran Church in Danville where my godchildren worshiped, relieved to sit anonymously in a church where the sandal-footed Zen Lutheran pastor, Steve Harms, offered extemporaneous wisdom, a heart for justice, and a dancing Christ. I met other exiles there: black South African church leaders, Nicaraguan villagers, ostracized gay pastors, lesbian couples, and even affluent people whose hearts had been renewed by radical acts of love. My church wounds began to heal. In return I tithed whole-hearted affirmation to the minister, wondering what it would have been like to receive the same.

But, I couldn't affirm what churches were doing to clergywomen. Ten clergywomen and I gathered each month in West Oakland. I hoped to revive the joy in our bodies. Unfortunately, most of them were barely hanging onto their lives. Queens of cordiality, they smiled, got to the studio and passed out. Three young women still laughed easily and expected friendship. The body language of the older women, whose eyes peeled back in their heads like extras in *The Exorcist*, seemed to snarl, "I'm only here for myself."

One woman dreamt that she was in a concentration camp, trying to help row upon row of bony bodies stacked in bunks. Outside an open door was a lush garden. But, she couldn't move. She had become a skeleton too.

I tried to tell the women, "You can't bear everyone's sorrow in your body. Play with me. I've learned an easier way to get where we want to go. What good is religion if you are miserable?" They eyed me with trained willingness. But it was clear that the only thing that could help them was direct transfusions of rest. Playfulness took energy.

Two women stopped coming. One transferred to a non-clergy group.

It occurred to me that I, too, had lost faith that clergywomen could be happy and I wasn't offering real answers. They couldn't leave their jobs. Until I regained neutrality about the church, I couldn't do any transformative work with them. I heard, "Cynthia, heal your lack of enthusiasm for the church."

At Wing It! practice, with an opportunity to do a solo dance, I told the company that I needed to retrieve my enthusiasm for the church. As soon as I began, I felt the old boiler of pain in my chest break down. Before long I was chanting the cry, "I love the Church. I love the Church. I love the Church." Kathunk! Kathunk! Kathunk, went the boiler. Ready to blow, my words turned into screams. I yelled at the walls, "You don't understand. I LOVE THE CHURCH!"

KA-BOOM!!!

Afterwards, I tried to sort out what had happened. Conjuring up a blank movie screen in front of my eyes, I saw a long, gray, impenetrable, stone wall appear. A medieval religious community full of my family and friends lived inside the wall. I knew the story. I was accused of jeopardizing them. Frustrated and unable to convince them otherwise, I was forever shouting to them, "I love you. I love you. I love you."

Whether the medieval community was fictitious or an emblem of a wound didn't matter. I needed healing. Two days later, as I tried to dance again to heal my lack of enthusiasm for the church, I couldn't move. Phil got up. He held me and the relief was immediate. I closed my eyes, and saw the wall. This time my people walked through it toward me. My spirit was still in them. I saw that I had given my spirit to them only to have it cut off. Part of me was lost in them. It cost me my serenity.

I thrust my right hand out across time, life, and death, summoning all the inner fire I could. Calling my spirit home with a long, continuous plea of the heart, Phil held me to the ground. Single handedly, I retrieved my soul from those people.

Not until that moment did I realize that you could have a relationship to a people without giving them your soul. My body finally understood that it was possible to be in the church but not of it as I felt the entirety of my communal soul force back in my body again.

This was the first soul retrieval I performed. Later, I learned that it is rare to perform a soul retrieval for oneself. If not for five things, Phil's grounded presence, Wing It!, my wild imagination, dance, and believing in my weird self, it never would have happened. Who else could perform this service? Jesus performed soul retrievals, and no one in the church had a clue about what to do.

Once again I realized that there are wounds we cannot heal alone, particularly communal wounds. If a community hurts you, then community is necessary to heal that wound.

I would just as soon sleep through dreams, but when I was hand-ed a nightmare so full of puns and archetypes that even a symbolic dimwit could glean something from it, I had to pay attention. It began in an English church that had been turned into a museum. Tours were given to show off the old, ornate, three-foot long keys hanging on the walls. No one knew what they were for anymore.

I was there for a party to be held where the altar used to be. The front of the church looked as ordinary as any YMCA rec room. It had a ring of folding chairs, balloons, party hats, and friendly faces. People awaited the Host, my friend Michael, a dancing priest. Off to the side twelve chairs lined up in a row.

Someone complained, "Why aren't they in the circle?"

I retorted, "It's a party! It doesn't have to be so linear."

Suddenly, a black haired woman jolted. Her one-year-old child, Danny, sitting in a car seat near a pillar of the church disappeared. She panicked and ran through the museum crying, "Where's my child?"

I joined in the search. Behind the pillar, I saw a white Labrador retriever bound up the stairs that went down into the old school. The dog looked friendly. It must be O.K. to go down there. Downstairs in a room right under the chancel, below the party, I shined a flashlight into a giant pit toilet with side-by-side open stalls. I thought, "Good! I need to go to the bathroom." But, each toilet had a hole the size of a quarter. "My shit is bigger than that!" I thought. When I spied a canister with a wider mouth, I saw that it was full. No wonder they turned the church into a museum, I surmised. They didn't move the crap out.

The mother continued frantically searching for her child. I gave up the attempt to relieve myself and resumed searching. Beaming the flashlight down a corridor into a warehouse, loop upon loop of electrical wires and Christmas lights hung from the rafters. Much of the church lighting was in storage.

I heard a child cry out. Hiding behind debris, the mother and I crept forward until we saw a man. He walked toward us like a zom-bie. I noticed his face was in the shape of a pan and he was deadpan. He was on a mission but I was not afraid. He had no affect. As he passed us by, the child cried again.

Crouched down, I caught a glimpse of the mastermind, a woman. She had ratty eyes, soiled hair, and wore a disheveled blue, stained apron embroidered with one word, "Tuesday." "Tuesday's child is meek and mild?" Apparently no longer. The kidnapper was an abused woman, an overly domesticated anti-Madonna. She was dangerous.

She caught sight of me and raw instinct urged me on. I lunged and hit her. It was as if I had no force. I curled my fist and punched her. She bounced back like a punching bag. Picking her up, I threw her out of the church basement and down a hill. She rose again. I was filled with the extreme terror of one's worst nightmare as she came after me.

I awoke in sweat.

That morning I shared my dream with a women's group. A woman with a tender, matter of fact voice reminded me, "Cynthia, you can't kill the abused woman. You have to take her in your lap." And an unseen voice echoed old words, "The abused you will have with you always."

I thought about the damage done by the women behind the scenes in the last two churches. Abused and abusive women lurked in the shadows at the foundation of the church? Had the divine feminine turned on us all? Had she stolen the male child? Could I take the disempowered feminine into my lap even when she threatened me?

Friedrich Nietzsche said, "Whoever fights monsters should see to it that he does not become a monster himself." A secret monster lived in me. Its name was rage. In my life, several times a year a fury of sensations welled up so strong that I was tempted to jump out of windows. I slammed doors and drove angrily through the night. What are angry, frustrated women to do?

A middle-aged woman approached me at the conclusion of my seminary class. She was a victim of every kind of abuse: priests, her father, road workers, even lightening bolts. She begged me to heal her. Neon lights flashed. This woman needed a dozen soul retrievals. No one ritual, art form, spirit guide, or dance would be enough. To heal so much violation demanded a community. Besides, I never wanted to heal anyone. Should I take her into my lap? I had no intention to heal anyone, yet others seemed to find me capable of it.

I said, "Go and get two others and I will help you," hoping that would be the end of it. But that is what she did. I don't know if she received the healing she needed from me, but I began attracting more and more of this kind of thing. What do you do when you attract things you don't want? I was about to learn just how vulnerable and unskilled my healing gifts were.

On a beautiful spring day I drove up to the labyrinth to lead a class. At a red light, a homeless man crossed the street in front of me. His clothes, skin and the paper cup in his hand were the same shade of brown. He glanced over his shoulder at me. That was all it took. I felt a wave of energy penetrate and grab my life force.

"Hey!" I yelled. Fortunately, my windows were rolled up. As the light turned green I thought, "That's going to cost me."

Two hours later at the labyrinth, the afternoon wind picked up. I started coughing. At dusk the cough deepened. Fever and exhaustion enveloped me. That night, arriving at the emergency room, I passed out with full-blown bronchitis.

It took days to regain enough energy to think again. What happened? Slumped on my front porch, I looked across the street at the house with the unfortunate green paint job. The woman who lived there got into your business faster than anyone. I often hid from her. Should I take her into my lap? She reminded me of a neighbor back in Richmond who frequently knocked on our door when she found out we were ministers. One day an ambulance came. She had drunk herself to death behind closed curtains. It had been days before she was found. I still felt guilty about that.

I thought back to the homeless guy at the stoplight. Was I unconsciously poised to heal anyone? Was my healing energy chronically stuck in the on position? Wasn't that how good Christian women were supposed to behave, always available to help? I had to hide when I needed rest. Suburbia was the perfect hideout. No one bothered me except for lonely, needy neighbors. Love my neighbor? I couldn't. My healing energy was out of control. If only humans had a switch to control it.

Light bulb! I put my hand up in the air in front of me, imagining a light switch and turned my healing energy off. I turned my open, healing energy off. Between hacking coughs, I observed the grass fade to an ashen grey. I wanted to cry. Off wasn't good either. It felt like giving up life.

I stuck my hand in the air again and flipped the switch on and off, and on to off. My body responded enthusiastically. Having a choice to be a healer or not was all I needed.

⚘

One morning, as four-year-old Katie watched TV, I sidled up to her and asked, "Can I sit here?" She recoiled her legs and kicked me donkey style, full force.

I screamed, "You can't hit me!"

Terrified, she ran to her room crying. I plunked down, appalled at myself. In the little black book of mothering, I tattooed another "bad mommy." I hated it when anyone violated my space, hated my temper, and hated being out of control.

Determined to get to the bottom of my reactionary behavior I made another appointment with Phyllis. Seated across from her at her kitchen table, Phyllis began her reading and stiffened. "You're in trouble. Your record keeper is fuming. You keep messing around with your life records and interfering with her job. If you don't quit it she's going to leave." In Phyllis' cosmology, record keepers are like God's librarians, organizers of eternity's information highway. Updating each person's soul process they make it possible for us to forget about the past until the information is needed.

The scowl on Phyllis' face was threatening enough. I imagined my inner know-it-all sneaking off into the cosmic library stacks to steal and mislay various files. I've always insisted on snatching any information I could use to protect me from injury and humiliation. Even if no record keeper existed, Phyllis' psychic laser beam had once again zoomed in on a weak link in my soul, my desire to be omniscient. I hadn't even realized that I was playing God in that way.

I apologized saying, "I'm sorry. I promise to stop messing with my files." What a relief. I didn't need to know everything. It was somebody else's job. I could let it go.

Phyllis relaxed and turned her focus to the question of my defensive reactions. I prepared myself. Phyllis never coddled me.

In mere moments she said, "When you were conceived, another spirit wanted to be born in the same body, a boy, a brother. You had to compete for your own space. This is why competition is your first way of relating. He is still hanging around. Its time to move this brother out and connect him to God. You don't have to compete anymore." She helped reorganize my space and I felt better.

I left Phyllis' house, feeling like a woman who finally had her own room. I recalled that the Hebrew word for salvation could be translated, "room to walk around in." That's what it felt like in my skin. The vigilant battles to defend my space lost some fuel. As a result I became less threatened by feedback, critique, and raised eyebrows. I practiced staying soft inside, letting the energy of others pass through me. Sometimes I even laughed and said to life's scary things, "Touch me. Touch me. I love it when you violate my space."

At a pastors' conference in Orlando, Florida, I wasn't the only one who sounded like that spiritual dwarf, Grumpy. The talented conference leaders were critical and cynical. Instead of listening to the drone about what was wrong with pastoral leadership, I escaped with Phil to Universal Studios and rode roller coasters.

My ongoing prayer to restore enthusiasm for the church got its most memorable answer on the trip to Sydney, Australia where Trisha Watts and Rod Pattenden organized a conference called "The Body of Evidence." They laid down a huge canvas labyrinth. Conferees danced, walked, and crawled to the middle. When I got to the center, I shut my eyes. My feet drank up earth energy like ravenous, starved, thirsty tree roots. After years of throwing freelance spears toward the center of church and culture, trying to hook up institutional hearts with the far-out worlds of dance, play, body, and imagination, I felt like an edgy outcast. But this body of evidence told another truth.

"Take the center," came a neutral voice.

Hearing those words, the soles of my feet didn't hesitate another instant. There was nothing to fight. No more competition for center, no despair. I was at the center of my own faith: ordained, a minister, a dancer. I took authority from that and came to see that the dance of life is always the center, not just for me, but also for many.

Enthusiasm in the Greek means to be filled with God, centered, and full. I was in the place known by poets, mystics, and tribal people as The Great Dance. As C.S Lewis wrote in *Perelandra,* "The Great Dance does not wait to be perfect until the peoples of the Low Worlds are gathered into it. We speak not of when it will begin. It has begun from before always. There was no time when we did not rejoice before God's face as now. The dance which we dance is at the center and for the dance all things are made. Blessed be God!"

A woman came to see me in search of joy. Willing to assist her I called on Christ. He showed me a tarnished antique vase that must cost a universe and handed it to me saying, "Hold it."

I took it and felt its heft, afraid of dropping it. Were my hands trustworthy?

Then he whispered, "Dance with it."

Dance? I am notorious for creating messes. My mother put me in dance class because I knocked into so many things. But, it was true. When I dance my body, space, and time make sense of the world. Instead of being all arms and legs, my actions become cohesive, graceful and transformative. Maybe Jesus was right. I am more trustworthy when I dance.

I began dancing with the woman, slowly encouraging her to do the same. She, too, had been violated and lost faith in her body. Dancing together allowed us to carry our own priceless vessels and move with greater love. We met for a year. She regained energy, strength, and joy.

Dance is a powerful form of spiritual direction. There have been times when I've moved too quickly or too slowly with people and the precious contents threaten to leap out of my hands. I've even injured a couple of athletic men by presuming them to be stronger than me. Thank goodness soul healing isn't dependant on exactness. The mysterious dance of life works is best medicine when we, in common willingness, risk the beauty of simple partnership. As Jean Clayton's poem, "The Friendship," says so well:

> *There is only dance*
> *through the changing of place;*
> *so one day you are the healer,*
> *and the next the wounded child,*
> *and by turns it*
> *is my time to be*
> *lost and find*
> *home in your eyes,*
> *or to give you a*
> *flower of peace.*
> *Solemnly we join*
> *the pace, learning*
> *the steps in silence,*
> *each*
> *wondering if the*
> *other hears and feels*
> *how tender,*
> *how like a strong*
> *river*
> *is the tune.*

Easter Sunday I wept. Hundreds of people filled a sanctuary, singing about the impossibility of a dead man walking away from an empty tomb. I knew more about this than twentieth century people dare to admit. This man lives. This man remembers me. This man speaks to me. Ludicrous faith, ridiculous belief! I believe in resurrection of the dead, in changed lives, in dying for others. Sunday school made it sound so easy. But, it is not. By faith I fly upside down, move when others sit, laugh in thick silence, and cling to God's dance like a life raft, willing to go down with it.

The Easter Jesus, ever leveraged against tradition's tombstone gave it another cracking push. I heard the church groan, "We can't move!" But, in time we will. For to dance in church is to change the world.

I'm glad my Jesus isn't jealous. Once I could confidently say I have a personal relationship with you know you, alternate guides started appearing in myriad forms. The myth of monotheism asserts that once Jesus is your man, you are to "have no other Gods." My Jesus acted more like a mother bird pushing her chick out of the nest.

Isn't the cosmos alive with divine dancers? Look at Michelangelo's Sistine Chapel, Hildegard of Bingen's illuminated mandalas, and St. Gregory of Nyssa's mural of dancing saints in San Francisco. Heaven teems with help. Every single one of us probably has a legion of cosmic nurses' aids. If anything I am beleaguered by divine help.

I found a power animal at the Goodwill while hunting for Wing It! costumes. Foraging through racks and racks of clothes, I grabbed a black T-shirt. A white hand-painted hummingbird lurched into the air. I don't know how I recognized it, but I knew that the little bird that fascinates people with lunatic energy and zooming zapping carried the spirit of my soul. I thought my medicine would be more like tiger or bear. But as usual the joke was on me. Surprise and humility are generally the confirmation of spiritual truth.

> *Dart, dance,*
> *How does she do it?*
> *Too miniature to fetch fear,*
> *"Look!" they say,*
> *predicting her disappearance.*
> *By instinct,*

she targets their nectar.
Eye of hummingbird
to heart of the flower,
poising, she plunges.
Direct hit.
Surgical intervention.
Eyes flash.
It only takes a second.
Plunge, extract, fly on.
Vampire of love
extracting so much good.
So many flowers.
So little time.

The hummingbird is also a kamikaze warrior. I watched a dozen of them fight over a flowered hedge in what I thought was a mating dance. But, someone informed me that their violent interpenetrations were territorial attacks. Joy is not the hummingbird's only medicine.

At age thirty-five my hair turned grey. By age forty I was a survivor of visions, voices, storms, deaths, deep waters, and the ecstatic dance of life. I was changed. You could see it in pictures. People said, "Gosh, that doesn't look like you. Your voice sounds different." I had traveled from being Cindy, which means light, to Cynthia which means daughter or goddess of the Moon, she who lives in the dark.

InterPlay was on its way to becoming an international community art practice. People the world over were losing their sense of dance, innate joy, and body wisdom. Many were lonely and isolated. Yet, by asking them to bring the palm of their hand to a partner's palm, social reunification happened. Stress evaporated. When people heard that they didn't have to articulate their body wisdom in order to have it, they relaxed. Talk was a tyrant. People needed something simpler and more direct to restore their soul.

I'd confirmed for myself that mainstream American religions don't teach from the whole book of human wisdom. Was this why my assignment had been "to bring together dance and religion?" So I could see what was missing? I was learning about shamanism through the back door of my own faith. Convinced that it wasn't crazy to hear voices anymore, I wanted skill, choice, and a healthy ethic for using the intuitive gifts of clairvoyance, the ability to see clearly, and clairaudience, the ability to hear more than is being spoken. I gathered a circle of women to study with Phyllis Magal and we made monthly trips over five years to her home north of San Francisco to practice the tools of body wisdom. We read energy, deciphered and took responsibility for anything that we projected as an image, and learned to account for presences and absences in each other and ourselves.

I kept all this semi-secret. I didn't want to be known as clairvoyant. I only wanted to refine my ways of knowing. I knew that journeying into psychic realms could remove me even more from mainline western folk. I both did and didn't care. In that half-lit place between what I'd been told is true and what I'd learned for myself, I garnered courage to name my own reality. If I didn't, others always would. I scoured the dictionary in search of my job title and found Mystagogue—"a leader initiated in mysteries"—and Mysteriarch—"one who presides over mysteries." From my search I collaged two other words into Choreo-transducer to mean "one who dances to transmit power from one system to another." From this I wrote my job description, so at least I know what I do.

Seize ancient books of wisdom
prowl uneasy caverns,
glean secret knowledge,
throw treasures deliriously
into the silver bowl of life with a clatter.

Uncover discarded ecclesiastical relics
and ornate, dust-thick tablets
entitled salvation, grace, eternal life.
Trace their roots back to

flesh, spit, mud, breath, and joy.
Transform the forgotten keys
that open gates of spirit
back into ordinary house keys.

In prayer halls of dance
scrutinize raw data, research
this divine encyclopedia,
the body.

Enroll in tutorials with
sacred dancers, godsons,
angels, hummingbirds,
Mennonite psychics,
African spirits, and the Tree of Life.

Practice spiritual disciplines
like fall, rise, shake,
balance, breathe, let go.
Uphold sacred irreverence
the right to laugh
no matter what authorities say.

Leap rational walls
construct healing routes that
resurrect physicality.

Usher in dance, story, stillness.

Maintain a mystic's curiosity.
Concoct rituals.
Chase lost energy.
Return to former lives.
Coordinate reunions of body and soul.
Shoot rapids, take to the stars.

Make peace with having
nothing, no time, nobody,
no place, and nothing to say.

Dance circles around suffering:
abuse, murder, expulsion,
divorce, obsession,
disease, accusation.
Handle blades of rage,
knives of clarity, and
the power to kill off.

Dream and translate dreams.
Master technologies.
Teach rapture.

Sell wisdom,
talk on the phone,
ask for money and
seek the terrified, crazy,
advanced human beings
who no longer fear being called silly.
Made visible by humility's kiss
look for their eyes shining in
the dark fields of unknowing.

Honestly, I was ready for spiritual boot camp to be over. Instead I learned that to prepare for mid-life you have to be ready to have your psychic roof to cave in. I was ready to enter what mystics call the "dark night of the soul." Or, in my case, what medical professionals called dysthymia, a.k.a. the "d" word, depression. At the time I had no clue that so many spiritual teachers were afflicted with it: Henri Nouwen, Mother Teresa, beautiful human beings who talked to God, got big bangs of divine love as the recipients of clear messages about how to serve. In my case, I was now a candidate for mystical dis-enlightenment whether through my peri-menopausal road bumps or my ancestral pre-dispositions. I was set up for the BIG D.

I considered myself a high-functioning community member, a bright spot on the planet. OK a bit too bright. One counselor teasingly called me, "Saint Cindy." I don't think it was a compliment. She carefully suggested I might be depressed. How could that be? I'm an irrepressible, energetic thruster. Thruster is the name ascribed to one of four movement dynamics in what I call the Meyers Briggs of Movement. Two kinesiologists and an innovative dance educator named Betsy Wetzig discovered that we each are most at home in swinging, thrusting, shaping, or hanging. When I was a pastor, a friend administered a simple arm test, maneuvering my arm in a circle. Feeling my limb take on a life of its own, she definitively pronounced, "You're a thruster. Using energy is how you relax."

Thruster? What woman in a helping profession wants to be called a thruster or an in-your-face, overly-direct, ambitious, go-getter with too much to do and too much to say? A pushy not-so-broad broad? Yikes. Spiritual people reek of quiet, harmonious love, especially women of God. Only Goddesses from colorful cultures are warriors.

I felt both relief and alarm. I had tried hard to subdue this part of me and lived in fear of my power. Was it my nature? On one hand I wanted to make peace with myself. On the other hand, being irrepressible, exuberant, and expansive were problematic. I blurt things out, speak intensely and too much, and jump before anyone else sees what's coming. My eyebrows furrow. I get pokey, pointy, and lose myself in looking OUT. I squeeze my arms against my sides to prevent them from knocking things over. I hold my breath to subdue the excitement I channel into energetic non-stop work. My ability to hang out, loll, or meander was nil until I exhausted myself.

Pushing my thruster down was dangerous. It caused me to work double time and eventually got so bad that if I went into my kitchen I was overcome by a surreal attraction to knives accompanied by an unnatural desire to stick them in me. I wasn't suicidal. This was something else.

How do you embrace being both a thruster and a forty-year-old mom praying everyday for the courage to be non-violent? I'm more warrior than mom. When someone said, "A monk is a warrior who has put down their sword," I wondered how I could put down a thing that I had never held in my hands?

One day I enacted taking my power in my hands like a sword. Getting a handle on power frightened me. I didn't want to hurt anyone, myself included. I wanted to choose when and how to wield my thrust. It became clear why I needed to actively dance and sing my prayers. Like an athlete, movement was not an option. Moving is as necessary to my spiritual well being as playfulness is to my intensity. Ask my daughter. I'm a different person when I lighten up, move, take deep breaths and let them out with audible sighs.

Between thrusting and my inherited insistence on staying high, I pushed my adrenal glands right up the mountain of my thirties until I couldn't do it anymore. Summating my fortieth year, my metabolism suddenly dropped like a car battery losing its charge. The whole biological system ratcheted down in a moment in my first official aging spurt. Kathunk. All I could say was "Uh-oh."

But the truly devastating drop off in my energy hit on a triple threat day: Friday the 13th right before Easter, Bad Friday, just two days before tax day. Stephen and I couldn't pay our bills. On top of that Stephen told me that he planned to take another job as a pastor. More than ready to put down the breadwinner role, I let go and started crying. The next day I was still crying as my energy drained away faster than tears. My legs went leaden. I got into the bathtub and had my first seriously suicidal thought. Death seemed easier. I knew I was depressed. That very day I called and got an emergency appointment with a psychiatrist and got some medication. Depression is not something I wanted to mess with. I'd seen it in action in the lives of those I love. The disease locomotors in a downward spiral and like cancer, if not treated quickly and with due respect, would take you to places no human wants to visit.

Welcome to mid-life. No angels. No white lights. No strange voices unless you count that sound of a disembodied baby's cry coming from my chest cavity. Where was God?

Neither dance or InterPlay saved me from depression, but at least they gave me a road to get through it. I practiced "fake" hanging out as I let the medication do the difficult serotonin re-uptake inhibitor

pull-ups. I didn't try to get better. I sat in the sun, somehow miraculously avoided the pit of shame, and created stuff. I wrote poems
and thought about publishing them under a title like "Dancing on
the Dark Side of the Moon, (Would Anyone Like To Read My
Depression Poems?)" Frankly, some poems had more life in them
than I did.

> *bearing down on air*
> *nothing there*
>
> *no cash flow, no structure*
> *no way to build up*
>
> *rappel, reveal, repel,*
> *my aircraft went down*
>
> *its old party of possibility tumults as*
> *new recruits for a war zone took their seats.*
>
> *a dark skinned stewardess*
> *held the mike to amplify the bad news*
>
> *"don't panic, we are going to die."*
> *I look out the window.*
>
> *"die?" I scream as*
> *the plane arrests in midair.*

The good thing about depression is that it casts shadows where
shadows should be. Instead of denial's light, I started to see life as
the shady deal it is. I flipped my lifestyle on its back and surveyed
the underbelly of all that had been promised to this white, middle
class woman. It was a seriously mixed bag.

I

Suburban mystic
I walk the cloisters of
Penney's, Target, and Safe Way
buying frozen yogurt, socks, tortillas,
as I pray for the world.
Minivan hermit in a Mitsubishi confessional,
I scream, cry, dither, dream and
stick plastic cards in machines
gassed up for car pool tunnel syndrome,
chronic fatigue,
and the insane drive to find myself.

II

I rent two bedrooms
that I can abandon at will
never saying good-bye
to the lady next door.
Remember her?
What was her name?
Till then, I lock my screen,
unobtrusively smiling at the gardener,
mail carrier, you,
inheriting the grand prize:
independence and freedom's promise
"You can do anything."

III

I descend from those who
snipped off the past like
so many ancestral dead ends,
left old countries, empty plates,
and darkened dreams,
putting their visionary hands
to this bright blank canvas
the United States of Anonymity.

A caretaker of their will to forget,
I mourn and don't know why.

IV

Daughter of no story,
family Bible burnt in a Midwest barn,
I go to the mailbox dying for postcards,
addicted to meetings, workshops,
church, PTA.
I scatter old photos on the floor,
ancestral, mute lives
poking me in the ribs
daring me to admit I
starve for tribe and land.

V

Mystic on Broad Way
I am in awe of great-grandma's
transatlantic passage to
land a job as a cleaning lady
paving the way for
generations of dirty laundry
until Dad rode the wave called
the Korean War, the GI Bill,
and finally bought the soldiers
split-level house
bequeathing me the sacred family words,
"Be whatever you want."

VI

Inheritor of shattered remnants,
the family china,
a stack of bibles and
lingering dreams of
rituals, dances, farms,
America is mine but it is

Hispanics, Africans, and Asians
that retain songs wealthy with spirit
while I grope for an ancestral dance
and despise the legacy born of
this demon, dominance.

6 | *Pushing Up the Sky*

*Cool, unlying life will rush in, and passion will make
our bodies taut with power, we shall stamp our feet with
new power and old things will fall down, we shall laugh,
and institutions will curl up like burnt paper.*
—D. H. LAWRENCE

THE MILLENNIUM WAS ON THE DOORSTEP. How could I say
no when two distinguished professors and a talented doctoral student invited me to collaborate on an original musical at the Graduate
Theological Union? We wrote *Push Up the Sky* as an ensemble piece
for fifteen characters thrown together by fate. We imagined them in
route to the remote Marquises Islands where each character's racial,
political, and religious dilemmas would be exposed as they revealed
their purpose for the trip. Under the wing of an island guide, some
of their good intentions would crumble, but the spirit of community would prevail.

I had no idea we were launching a Titanic.

Students were auditioned and cast. Five white people, three
African Americans, and a Vietnamese woman filled lead roles. Less
experienced performers included a woman from India, Germany, a
Chinese-American woman, and two Euro-American women. They
were cast as Sky Dancers.

It was an ambitious undertaking. The play was never work-
shopped. With only one class per week we planned to perform in

147

the spring. Two seminarians who were recent escapees from New York's musical theater scene, had a they-don't-know-what-they're-biting-off look in their eye. That was the least of our worries.

By the end of the first month the lead woman told us she was troubled. Over the piano after rehearsal, she questioned several of our artistic choices: our invention of a shamanic tour guide with an alcohol problem, our use of natives to save white people, our appropriation of the title "Push Up the Sky" from a Pacific Island myth, and our unconscious use of one of colonialism's themes—traveling to exotic places to "help" indigenous people. Having already clocked weeks of personal time to create the musical, we were dumbfounded and clueless about how to navigate these challenges. I had never analyzed this or any play from colonialism's perspective. What about the other values in the play?

The next week she quit and sent her written complaint to the president of the Graduate Theological Union. Anxiety about this and other issues broke out in the cast like a rash. As we struggled to rehearse as well as listen a cast member and former lawyer wrote to the administrators of Pacific School of Religion "to interrupt the racism in the play." The ex-lawyer refused to share her letter with me. How was I, the ignorant oppressor supposed to learn from my mistakes if I wasn't included in the exchange?

At the last rehearsal before a workshop performance, she too quit. I wept in frustration. I watched the breath go out of the musical director who was a veteran of numerous professional plays. The professor who had initiated the play got chest pains and had to quit. Several talented students dropped out. Over the winter break my school administrators canceled sponsorship of the play. No one talked to anyone, but everyone wanted change NOW! Unfortunately, group bodies don't work that way. I had experienced such mutinies in the local church but never in the arts or academia.

Standing amidst the wreckage, I phoned the seminary president. "Was I being punished? Hadn't I taught for a decade at the school? I was an alumni!" Why couldn't they talk with me before taking these actions? I was angry with myself. I had studied liberation theology. I embraced stories of diverse people. Was I this clueless?

Hitting bottom, at least I was still thrashing. So I grabbed my little life raft called InterPlay, hung onto the encouragement of friends who were people of color and with the two remaining faculty invoked the oath of the theater, "The show must go on." We transplanted the play to another seminary, revised the script, and ratcheted down our ambitions. *Push Up the Sky* was performed in three cities. The seminary president saw it and thanked the people of color who performed. He didn't thank me.

More than the play needed repair. Relationships were injured and I still didn't understand how I had contributed to so much pain. I got the help from two anti-racism consultants to review the script and emails and share what they saw.

I committed to heal what I could by meeting with deans, presidents, the people of color caucus, and the woman who gave us the first harsh critique. She and I met with the Asian dean. As I listened I observed their weariness.

Finally I visited the ex-lawyer. In her living room she told of her journey as a Southern daughter of a racist minister, her father. She knew what racism looked like and had no tolerance for it. In her opinion I was not evil but I was part of something that was. I barely grasped her words, my racial fog still dense even after studying about racism, feminism, gay freedom, and having taught for years in the most liberal, albeit white, seminaries in the world.

The semester ended. I lost touch with most of the participants except the music director. It was years before he could write music again.

I hate shame so much that I will do anything to avoid it. Determined to override it, I logged hundreds of hours researching how to heal racial pain. Other questions plagued me too. Like, how had a person with pastoral gifts flunked out of ministry? And why did I feel belittled when people called me a dancer? What was my purpose if not to dance?

Questions like these are provocateurs of initiation. And every initiation is physical. To exchange an old idea for a new one is bodywork. The questions that arose had to do with my directive, "clarity of vision." What was I doing and why was I doing it? Little did I know that to gain such clarity is like trading in a VW for a jet. Ready or not, I was about to move into higher gear.

Dance came easy. It was as effortless as the grapefruits that fell from the tree outside my kitchen window. The tree blotted out the sun and dumped tart, yellow orbs year round until they rotted in a steamy stew. Like these grapefruits, dance was my nature, my gift, and my rot.

A gift needs to move, or, like fruit, ferments at our feet. Not a pretty sight.

One day I decided to tackle those overabundant grapefruits. I got out the big black trash bags and tried to haul one to the curb. How would the trash guys lift hundreds of pounds of rotting grapefruits? My next strategy was to place an attractive bushel on the curb with a free sign. When no one took any, I tried going door-to-door, asking "Would you like some grapefruits?" The neighbors glared back at me. We lived in an old grapefruit orchard. But, to the Irish priests and nuns I shared a massage class with the grapefruits were a pot of gold at the end of the rainbow. They couldn't believe their good luck.

"Do you want more?"

"Is the pope Catholic? Yes! Bring us more!"

I don't enjoy my own gifts the ways others do. A brilliant thinker, poet, computer wiz, or vocalist can take us places that we'll never get to on our own.

That's why we get called.

I have visionary friends who are too good at office work. They are asked to administrate organizations and do accounting. It's a call, but it's not their purpose. Occasionally, they leave these jobs to risk everything to audition, travel, or learn an art like spiritual direction. Something pushes them to go places that are nowhere as easy or natural as their gifs.

Even the Divine calls on our gifts. "YOO HOO. DANCE AND RELIGION. CAN YOU GET IT TOGETHER?" Thankfully, a call is not a command. When I knelt on the floor of my Culver City apartment and offered to hold dance and religion together, I was more than willing. But, was it my true-life purpose?

No one will beg you to fulfill your purpose. You may not even be able to accomplish it much less articulate it. Worse, you may not even have a knack for it. Nonetheless, it's our central hunger and guides our every move.

I met a musical theater performer for whom singing was a gift. But, singing didn't satisfy him. He wanted to make music. When auditioned for a musical, accompanying himself on guitar, the auditioner said, "Try again but lose the guitar." It pained the performer. His father, who was also a musician, always discouraged him from playing music since there was no money to be made at it. In spite of this, the man quit musical theater and opened a music studio. Playing music was his purpose.

Someone said, "Use the talents you possess: for the woods would be very silent if no birds sang except the best." Dance may be a gift, but I knew it was connected to something else buried in my bones that wanted out.

Having never studied political science, leafleted, or served a campaign, I was surprised when the 1999 U.S. Presidential elections illuminated my life purpose. The contest between George Bush and Al Gore made even the politically skittish think.

At an InterPlay gathering, Phil had us "babble" for thirty seconds about the election. It poured out that I was afraid that if George Bush won, the civil rights of gays and lesbians would be endangered, affecting many of my dearest companions. I hated it when anyone was prohibited from expressing his or her nature. Down below my election fears I found something more, an unstoppable desire for freedom. It's the very dream that the United States is founded upon: freedom of speech, freedom of religion; the dream that many an American will fight for.

Overnight I clarified my purpose: *to foster freedom for all people.* Five words that rang true like a navigational bell. Freedom isn't natural. In fact, I am tempted to control everything and everybody. But when I employ my gifts for creativity, dance, and InterPlay it comes easier. Questing for freedom enlivens me. It is a challenge that I can pursue for a lifetime.

As soon as I articulated my purpose things started happening. Inner communications moved from dial up to high-speed broadband. My ear and heart attuned to forecasts of change. In the studio, I used kinesthetic imagination to take the institutional church out of my body. A huge medieval building appeared. At its cornerstone, a tree grew like a giant burl. It was the tree of life. Isadora Duncan's words sprang to mind. "You were once wild here, don't let them tame you."

Then in a dream a Chinese master introduced me to my new teacher, a woman about my age named Kathy. As he departed he gave me a final exercise. "Lean backward, past the point of holding yourself up. Then return to standing." When I tried, it was impossible. Kathy then demonstrated and I tried again. I leaned back and found muscles I'd never used, muscles outside of my body. As I pulled back upright, the monks who witnessed me said, "Ooooh."

Weeks later at Isis Oasis, a retreat center dedicated to the Egyptian goddess, where artistic wildness is regularly unleashed, I dreamt that I heard knocking on my bedroom wall.

"What is it?" I asked.

"Biblical logarithms," came the answer.

That day it was a riddle I asked everyone, "What's a biblical logarithm?"

Finally, a guy talking on the phone to his wife back in Minneapolis asked her, "Honey, do you know what a biblical logarithm is?"

From two thousand miles away she answered spontaneously, "That's easy. It's the sound of trees singing. Log-a-rhythm. Get it?"

Emailing friends about my dreams one woman suggested the exoskeletal muscles that helped me stand upright were other people. Another wondered if "the muscles outside our body are our ancestors and the ideas in our hearts yet to be birthed." She wrote, "Whatever the muscles are, they connect us in prophetic ways."

A friend coincidentally named Kathy suggested that "being pulled upright by outside strength sounded like a transition from power over introduced by masculine masters to power with demonstrated by feminine wisdom. This required trust."

Anita, a Mennonite minister wrote, perhaps, the most prophetic words of all.

> Institutions and trees growing side by side are both organic living creatures, one more clearly organic from the earth, which for me is a matriarchal, earth/body-centered symbol. The building is more patriarchal, yet still organic, formed of and by people, a symbol of information, logic, reason, and intellect. We need both, that which is coming (the ancient body wisdom, the sacred earth traditions) and that which is beginning to crumble, because it doesn't work on its own anymore.

> Your work in institutions is not blatant or overtly confronting to the powers that be, yet subversive and powerful nevertheless. They let you in the door to balance the yin/yang, masculine/feminine. Students, sent out into what I see as the "medieval" world of religion (the forms of institutionalized religion haven't really changed since then, even the inquisition still goes on, maybe in more subtle ways). Starving for more earth/body-centered ways, they too must find ways to become Bridgers. The next millennium will be the arena for powerful shifts in the ways we do religion/spirit.

> The muscles outside the body strike me as what Gary Zukov, author of Seat of the Soul, calls multi-sensory perception, the development of our eighth chakra and beyond. It is the ability to communicate faster than our body can, a highly developed sense that allows people to become very advanced spiritually. If it were my dream, it could mean I'm moving into uncharted territories with lots of information about living in a world where reason, logic and intellect is failing (how far we THINK the body can bend). We need to rely more on our extra-sensory spiritual muscles for the truth. If it were my dream, it

could indicate moving into a place to receive informa-
tion about the collective vision, dream, and hope for
spiritual survival. Cynthia, it's a place you've been pre-
pared for well. Bridging body-spirit information in a
world that doesn't know where to begin, because they
have only known what they see, feel and touch. You
know both.

Images of the Tree of Life and the sound of trees singing got my attention. I remembered the giant pine tree that stood at the center of Isis Oasis. Dr. Suess said, "I speak for the trees, for the trees have no tongues." Amber Walker was more than happy to be an associate of Dr. Suess. A daughter of a midwife who lived amongst Santa Cruz mountain redwoods, she enlightened me about the placenta.

On my windowsill, I have a placenta print. It is a
print on paper that my midwife made shortly after
Mahri's birth. She pressed paper to the entire placenta,
and the resulting artwork is miraculous. It is a tree. The
cord makes the trunk of the tree, the veins are the ex-
tending branches, and the tissue becomes the leaves. The
placenta is the most powerful organ known to humans;
it has more functions and capabilities than any other, yet
it is the only temporary organ. It triggers a momma's
body to do what it must for the baby, it sustains the baby
while in the mother, it carries all of the cellular commu-
nication between mom and baby, it then triggers lacta-
tion, and then its work is done. It creates, teaches, sup-
ports, sustains, nurtures, and then dies. We all were con-
nected to this tree. This tree is where we came from. It
was the first tree to feed our bodies. I believe it carried
psychic communication between our mothers and us. Is
it any wonder I live in the Big Trees? Redwood trees grow
in families; circles. The "fairy rings" of Redwood trees
are held up by a community of roots. Underneath the

ground, in the moist darkness, the roots of all the trees in the ring intertwine and weave together. Redwood trees also have the ability to grow from their own wounds. When a tree gets a wound, a broken limb or a cut in its trunk, a swirling mass of wood forms over the wound called a "burl." This burl gives birth to new trees. Entire trees grow from wounds and support the trees they come from.

Like Ezekiel's dry bones coming back to life, invisible extrasensory communal muscles were quickly taking on flesh. We couldn't see it, but we were beginning to feel and name it.

My first mystical encounter with the Tree of Life happened in 1979 while performing Wayne Rood's *OmegAlpha*. Carol saw the Archangel Michael at the back of the church. Michael in the Book of Genesis is said to guard the Tree of Life. The final words of the Book of Revelation foretell a new city at the center of which stands the Tree "with its twelve kinds of fruit, yielding its fruit each month; and the leaves of the tree are for the healing of the nations." Beneath this Tree, the Bible promises, "there shall no more be anything accursed." I heard for the first time that this Tree offers a way of life.

Twenty years later, with freedom as my compass and tracking the Tree of Life, I met a woman who was so psychically sensitive that she had to live high on a mountain far away from people. When the woman looked at me she saw an icy woman inside me, a spirit from a northern lake. She surmised that I had summoned her for protection. I sensed the chilliness at my center. When she suggested I rely instead on the dozens of little birds surrounding my aura, she didn't know that my core community was named Wing It!

As I released my cold shoulder and too-coolness, the woman gave me these instructions, "follow a little green man into the woods to a large stump, take amber, eat mushrooms, and sit on the stump for as long as you need." I wasn't sure what it meant but it sounded restful.

I meditated on the meaning of all this. A family fable said that some of my ancestors arrived in the U.S. and stayed in a fallen tree. Their name was Stumpf, German for stump. Another story recounted the grandfather who fell from a beam at Delco Electronics in Indiana, avoided the hospital, and went to the mountains instead. After that he never got "out of the woods." His tombstone reads, "He loved mountains." Meanwhile my dad's favorite occupation is running through forests to clear trails and put on hundred mile mountain races. Trees are family blood medicine.

In search of the tree, I didn't expect to find it in the living room of a body worker. Selah helped people restore their Kundalini energy, the life force that runs up and down our trunk. Early trauma and "good girl" training had blocked and deadened my gut and hips. Selah suggested a breathing exercise called "the big draw." Falling way down into a long inhale and exhale, followed by twenty quick breaths, I exhaled a long hiss, contracted into my pelvis and then finally released. As I repeated this sequence, I offered my groin an intention of self-love and lay still, my arm resting over my face. Out of nowhere a huge tree of life appeared. I was sheltered between its roots.

Research reveals that the World Tree is a universal symbol. Buddha was enlightened under one. Sundancers do a sacrificial dance around one. Celts worshiped amidst them. Christians place the tree that became the cross at the center of worship. The Jewish menorah is also a tree.

The Torah begins at the foot of two trees, "Out of the ground the Lord God made to grow every tree that is pleasant to the sight and good food, the tree of life also in the midst of the garden, and the tree of the knowledge of good and evil." After the snake incident the Hebrew Bible continues, "God drove out the man; and at the east of the garden of Eden he placed the cherubim, and a flaming sword which turned every way, to guard the way to the tree of life."

I discovered that the power and promises of the Tree of Life occur throughout the Bible. Ezekiel prophesied to the displaced Israelites, "On both sides of the river there will grow all kinds of trees for food. Their leaves will not wither nor their fruit fail, but they will bear fresh fruit every month, because the water for them flows from the sanctuary. Her fruit will be for food, and their leaves for healing." Proverbs, a book of wisdom, assures, "She (Wisdom) is a tree of life to those who lay hold of her; those who hold her fast are called happy." Psalm 1 sings, "Blessed is the man who shall be like a tree planted by the rivers of water that bringeth forth his fruit in his season; his leaf also shall not wither; and whatsoever he doeth shall prosper."

The Tree of Life is not just an image. It's life itself showing us how to bend, be grounded, hold our form, propagate, bear fruit, provide shelter, offer beauty worthy of praise, connect heaven and earth, and offer medicine.

To this day the final words of the book of Revelation haunt me. "...and the leaves of the tree are for the healing of the nations." What are these healing leaves? A Buddhist meditation teacher says that all the leaves in the forest represent the whole of knowledge, so much knowledge. A teacher gives the student just a handful of leaves and says, "This is all that I can give you, and this is all that you can hold. What is it in comparison with all the knowledge that there is in the whole forest! But this handful of leaves is enough. With it you have the key to the whole forest. You have all that you need."

An ecstatic song sung by the prophet Isaiah promises, "You shall go out with joy and be led forth in peace, the mountains and the hills will break forth before you, there will be shouts of joy and all the trees of the field, the trees will clap their hands."

Trees singing. Trees dancing. If songs were jewels, I'd hang a folk song that Amber taught me around my neck and never take it off.

> *Standing like a tree with my roots dug down*
> *My branches wide and open*
> *Down comes the sun, down comes the rain,*
> *Up comes the life to a heart that is open to be*
> *standing like a tree.*

✺

In the pitch black of Oz Farm, an organic apple farm in Mendocino County, my cabin mate and I were in pursuit of a bat. It scrambled under the bed, giving me time to ruminate on a mental bat caught inside my mind.

That day at the retreat I was leading, a Jewish woman took me aside. She resented it when I said that InterPlay was more Christian than many churches. She wanted no part of a Christian group.

Her reaction caused me to ask, "Was InterPlay my church?" Phil and I had specifically avoided theological language and imagery in creating InterPlay. We designed it as a basic approach for anyone trying to put body, mind, heart, and spirit together again. I shared all this with my cabin mate.

With bat broom in hand, peering into the dark under the bed, she asked, "So, you think of yourself as ordained?"

Her question took me off guard. I taught at a protestant seminary. I led church conferences. Still, I worked in sweatpants or dance shoes, not in a clergy robe. Many of my friends were theological gypsies in search of spiritual experiences too hard to come by in religious institutions.

Was I ordained? I remembered my initial questions about being set apart, a male invention that decreased mutuality in relationship. As a minister I'd been taught not to befriend church members, keep my hands off people, and avoid being too poetic or personal when preaching. I rebelled and distanced myself from the traditional clergy role. I used ordination to authorize a message about reuniting body and soul in the church.

A light turned on inside my head. In fact, the church was not the container for InterPlay. The world was. Ordination did not embody the common ground I shared with people. I was willing to do whatever I could to create more common ground.

I wondered, "Could I remove the idea of being ordained?" If thoughts like "I am a pastor" or "my work is ministry" were simply thoughts codified in my flesh, could I take them out?

Instinctively, I brought my hands to my head and put "psychic fingers" around the thought of ordination. Pulling the thought out of my head, I saw gothic arches, altars and inscriptions appear before my eyes. My head cleared, felt breezy. My own spiritual architecture looked more like a lanai, an airy, tropical, unenclosed shelter open to land, leaf, and sky. I took a deep breath and let my head and heart breathe.

The bat flew out from under the bed. My roommate, a Benedictine liturgical artist, swept it out the door with a pragmatic whoosh. Why not sweep outgrown identities out the door like bats that shouldn't be there? That night, like a spouse who knows a marriage must be rearranged or end, I began to change my Christian vow. I traded in words like pastor, ministry, call, Protestant, Christian, and church, for friend, community, work, playmate, and humanity. I staked out my playground as the one that stays close to the body, nature, and life.

My ordination wasn't gone. It takes more than the whisk of a broom to undo something that God and community hold together. I just whooshed it outside until I could figure out what to do with it. The next morning in the group, I noticed that the InterPlayers hands did not lay heavy on my head.

> *You who*
> *ruffle my hair,*
> *tousle my spirit,*
> *soothe my too hot eyes,*
> *smooth out the too wild thoughts*
> *You who pet, press, and charm*
> *my lucky moments,*
> *don't stop, don't ever stop.*
> *Because of you today*
> *I eat apples and belong.*

What divine irony to alter relationship to Christian ministry at OZ, an organic apple farm. Just like Isaac Newton's apple, on a certain day, at a certain time, a thought fell from the tree and changed my view of reality. As obvious as gravity, I wondered how I had missed that being a body is enough.

I had to relearn simple truths. Each person is a tree with limbs, trunk, and roots. Human brains, wombs, lungs, reproductive organs, and placentas are all trees of life.

✳

Susanne Langer asserted in a masterful work, *Philosophy in A New Key*, that architecture shapes cultural modes of relating to create "ethnic domain." Worship isn't just personal. It is communal. I wondered what space best instilled in people the values of the Tree and Dance of Life?

Having visited the Swiss church of Protestant reformer John Calvin I saw the results of his attempts to return biblical authority to people. He stripped the gilded, baroque imagery from the sanctuary walls. Color was banned. The church went through an ethnic cleansing. Calvin attempted to free biblical truth from its Catholic encrustations, but he kept the vaulted building. Eventually pews were installed so that people could listen to the man preach his sermons. New forms of idolatry were instituted in the shape of monotheistic, monotone, and monotony. Mono. Mono. Mono. Dance and pageantry were ushered out the door or fled to streets, woods, and that most welcoming venue, the pub. The Protestants lost their sacred dance, forgetting that in Hebrew "word" means enfleshed action.

Indigenous people had sacred sites, not buildings. Nature was the venue to honor the Tree of Life. I had to go outdoors.

Redwood Park in the Oakland hills had a walking path that meandered along a stream at the bottom of a ravine. Leading to a redwood grove called "Old Church" where the nineteenth century loggers decimated the old growth forest and set up a logging camp, only the chapel's cruciform foundation remained. Directly across from it a footbridge led to an amphitheater situated amidst elegantly arched California bay trees and redwood spires. There was a fire pit and plenty of space to move.

I began leading monthly pilgrimages past the old church. Groups of us would walk in silence, soaking up the nourishing quiet of trees, birds, sky, and dirt. When we arrived we did nothing for the first twenty minutes. Then we did InterPlay's simple warm-up and enjoyed walking, stopping, running, dancing, singing, breathing, and telling stories. Trees became hidden shrines and portals reconnecting our hearts to the earth.

Over the months we attuned to nature's synchronous offerings such as the day a hummingbird played at my shoulder and the time an American Indian friend joined us and an eagle flew five feet over our heads. Even in December's pouring rain, we were rewarded as we met the earth where she was, muddy and wet. The changing seasons, the honest beauty of animal, leaf, and weather convinced us that nature was the true, divine stage. The "Old Church" became home as I linked to creation through my love of this one place.

After we played we walked back to our cars, returning to casual talk and friendship. Isn't such an easy stroll amidst nature's beauty the image of the Garden of Eden? Why didn't I do this more often?

In a dream I grew a new spine. The Tree of Life reorganized my body. I was given a new way to stand. For this my pelvis, legs and feet had to change. I leaned on trees for guidance as different parts of my groin contracted and adapted. For a while I could barely open my legs. I developed plantar fasciaitis, inflammation of the connection tissue on the bottom of my right sole. I had to remain patient for I knew I was in a season of holy legwork and had to pay attention to grounding and support. As energy finally flowed through my legs, my groin released. I was weightier. Either that or I was just forty-five.

A Chinook Indian prayer says, "May all I say and all I think, be in harmony with thee. God within me, God beyond me, Maker of the tree." Standing like a tree, roots dug down, branches wide and open, isn't just good posture. Yogis take posture as central to their physical practice because right relation and power comes literally through the stands we take.

The Latin word for stand, *sistere*, is the root used in consist—to stand with; insist—to stand in; resist—to stand against; persist—to stand through; and subsist—to stand under. These are power stances. But my favorite "standing" word of all, *solidarity,* reminds me of redwoods. Solidarity simply means to stand alongside.

I learned that I must be born fully into myself, continuously releasing residual illusions and memories that tie me to parental forms and promises of structure and security. The path of freedom leads us to stand down in our soles and legs to literally withstand life's pain and pleasure.

On my twentieth wedding anniversary I dreamt that Stephen and I were in a little rowboat on the sea. Without discussion, Christ arrived, pulled up the anchor and carried it to the horizon. This was the exact opposite of my favorite folksong *"The water is wide, I cannot cross over it and neither have I wings to fly. I'll buy a boat that can carry two and both shall cross my love and I."*

Was my marriage ending? No. But, various older women taught me that partners are not anchors. They are often not even in the same boat. Lifetime partners are more like kayakers. Sometimes barely in view of one another we ride a wild river, one shooting ahead of the other, often afraid to take the next rapid. In the night, resting on the banks in each other's arms, we restore ourselves.

My long-term commitments to God, Stephen, Phil, InterPlay, and the church constantly plunged me into deeper waters of trust. David Schnarch, author of *Passionate Marriage* wrote, "Intimacy is not for the faint of heart," and that trusting someone else isn't the main goal for long-term relationships. The question is "Do I trust myself enough to love others?" Do I know what I want even if it is to love unreasonably, test the waters of life, **make th**ings, and enjoy creation?

With deeper roots, a stronger **spine**, and strength in my female center, I discovered that my **capacity** to love extends beyond getting hurt, and beyond my ability to **feel** or express it. Love and relationship are mysteries. I surrendered my need to know what brings or holds people together. But I was jealously grateful for any moment of sensate clarity about love's miraculous power.

Courage to love, one of my life directives, had become the every-day work of long-term relationship. Something extraordinary was at work. Radically changing more than the face of relationship, the very nature of the dance was changing.

In a dream set in the old west, I followed a fearless leader who lay down in a ditch on the side of the road, instructing me and other cohorts to do the same. Adam and Eve, the original couple, rode toward us with guns in hand. They were avengers, picking people off one by one, shooting them where they lay. I watched my leader literally disarm Adam, taking off his left arm, the arm that lashed out and annihilated offenders. Then, to my horror, the leader reached into Adam's chest and grabbed a piece of his rib, (the raw stuff for making a human), and reclined back in the ditch. I was furious and confused. When the leader stabbed himself in the chest with Adams rib, killing himself in sacrifice, I screamed. Eve, lay motionless in front of the leader.

"Was this the best my leader could do? Jesus Christ!" I thought upon waking. Clearly, something male was dying. Something female was yet to be born.

☙

On Ascension Day in the Christian Calendar, the psychic's words came true. I headed off to the woods with Amber. She wanted to show me a mother tree that lived on Redwood Empire Timber Company land fifty miles south of Oakland. Locals referred to her as The Blessing Tree.

Seven of us met Amber at an inconspicuous spot on the side of the highway near a Timber Company sign that said, "No Trespassing." My thoughts flashed on Julia Butterfly Hill who took up residence in the limbs or a redwood tree to keep the loggers away. I admired her.

Trudging, sweating down and up hills, jumping over muck, the pilgrims hiked. Finally, around a corner, the mother tree stood wait-ing, huge and silent. We gathered before her and one by one entered her hollowed out trunk, saying to each other, "it really feels different in here doesn't it?"

We sang songs and shared our reasons for coming. That's when it occurred to me that I wanted to serve the Tree of Life. But, all I could think to say was, "I came to be ordained by the tree." I rose. Standing at her massive base I was overcome. I knew the trouble a vow could cause. Would I have to be another Julia Butterfly Hill? I got on my knees and asked the tree what to do.

"It doesn't work that way," I felt the Tree reassure me. It didn't ask for anything except connection.

Amber remembered, "You were called into the tree, quiet, very quiet, boundaries blurring, the sound of the trees singing, merging, one strong body, becoming the body that stretches between earth and heaven." Then she too entered the tree and squatted inside feeling its energy filling her up. One with the tree, flowing upward into infinite dark blue, arm branches reaching upward, outward, Amber received this blessing.

> *This is a safe, loving, wise, body*
> *This is a safe, loving, wise, mother*
> *This is a safe, loving, wise, father*
> *Embrace. Breathe. Welcome home.*

Months had passed when Amber alerted us that a "pre-harvest inspection team" of timber operators, foresters, and fish and game employees planned to inspect land around the Blessing Tree. Local people increased visits and prayers at the tree. In a small niche someone placed a tiny circular candle, a rune stone meaning "gateway," a scroll of prayers, a goddess, and a shell. On my behalf, on the inner left side, Amber hung a rosemary herbal heart with a smaller heart inside of it. Hundreds of flower petals pooled and spilled out of her and onto the ground.

When the inspection team approached the tree, they were awestruck. Someone gasped, "There's a shrine in one of these trees!" In its presence they agreed, "We can't let these trees be cut down." There was no discussion.

The inspection team took its report to the Board of Supervisors, in the presence of hundreds of local people concerned about the Mother Tree. Miraculously, the Redwood Empire Timber Company agreed not to cut in that area.

Rabindranath Tagore wrote in Gitanjali #37, "I thought that my voyage had come to its end at the last limit of my power...that provisions were exhausted and the time had come to take shelter in a silent obscurity. But I find that thy will knows no end in me. And when old words die out on the tongue, new melodies break forth from the heart; and where old tracks are lost, new country is revealed with its wonders." My trials in local church ministry were not over.

Stephen had a third try at pastoral ministry. As before, people seemed to sincerely like him. He had learned a lot about the gentle art of dealing with church transitions, was a good preacher, and an excellent chaplain to the aging. Wanting to be with him and Katie, I took a deep breath and transferred my membership to his church. While sensing a heavy energy in the sanctuary, the way people sang in a whisper and never moved from their Sunday morning spots, I focused on their prayers, which seemed to travel straight to God. I was impressed by the lively Filipino contingency that sat on the left side of the church, and a growing group of kids.

In the third year a middle-aged woman arrived in search of an internship. Stephen welcomed her. It took her six months to wrap the community in a matriarchal cord, like a spider securing silk threads around her prey. Her allies were rule-oriented, discontent folk.

For the third time I watched a woman snag the seat of emotional power. Stephen believed women should have power and patiently listened giving her more authority than she deserved. When he saw that damage was being done and that she was creating antagonism in the congregation toward him, he asked her to leave. Her allies began blaming Stephen for the ills of the church. And, many of them shunned me.

If there is a post-traumatic stress disorder associated with church pain, we were its poster children. But, we weren't alone. Many ministers endure intense conflict. Perseverance in modern religious leadership requires that a leader have massive doses of spiritual direction, therapy, and an unshakable commitment to their community. Perhaps this is why churches stagnate. Ministers who survive an attempt at a hostile takeover or a mutiny don't want to go there again.

Stephen quit. I promised that if he ever took a church job again, he could say so long to me. But I still wasn't ready to quit our tradition all together. I started going to the church where Phil was on staff, a west coast protestant cathedral for esteemed faculty from UC Berkeley and the Graduate Theological Union. I was grateful to finally come home to a place where dance was embraced, gay and lesbian members were hired and wed, inclusive language wasn't an issue, and the current minister, Pat deJong, a woman, had once been my improvisation teacher twenty years earlier.

Charlotte Russell, the minister of membership, invited me to coffee. Asked about my journey with the church, I confessed my weary tale. Charlotte was the first and only church representative who ever asked what happened on my road through ministry. She wept with me.

On the Sunday morning that I joined, sobs poured forth as I sang "Gloria" with other new members. It was embarrassing. My wounds were mighty, yet I believed that to honor my Christian ancestry remained a crucial restorative practice. Ignoring, avoiding, or despising my own people was as bad as deforesting my homeland. Either that or I am just loyal to a fault.

In January 2001, at age 46, and in Australia again, after reading Emily Dickinson's poetry, I penned this self-prophesying poem before heading out to teach InterPlay with Phil:

Creation's bloom
and all of want
are born of dark
and lack and daunt.

Fertile soil is
earth's despair.
Rage and Heat
can be Repair.

Death upturns
the ruined loam,
declares and marks
its place as Home.

Refusers of the
great decay
won't break the churning
changed way.

Odd that all the LIFE
we fear
ferments in dark
chaotic Cheer.

The InterPlay gathering was held in an old church in the center of Sydney's gay community. The pews were gone and Australian InterPlayers had already broken in the wood floor. Rod, the minister of the church, an artist by nature and training, had been bitten hard by InterPlay. He kept bringing us "down under" each year, until he had a magnificent InterPlay community of his own.

That day something huge welled up in me. When I told Phil, he suggested that I dance. He invited workshop participants to gather and seat themselves. I grabbed a stick of black chalk and smeared it on my face. Phil put on drum music. I danced for fifteen minutes moving into a light visionary trance. Present to both inner and outer worlds, I observed myself exform old patterning from my patriarchal religious training. I saw a bridge between worlds being laid down. I took hold of my own joy. I sweated.

When I finished I had the familiar feeling of being strange even to myself. I laughed at the weirdness of it all and tried to reassure everyone, including myself, that I was not completely whacked out. By the end of the workshop I was so fatigued that Trish Watts took me to her healer.

With my head resting on the healer's table, she began her prayer. It was completely quiet when I heard her say, "I am being told not to touch you. The Archangels are present and a new blueprint is being laid down."

A deep peace overcame me. When I got up from the table I could barely walk. My energy seemed to be the size of a fetus. Was I literally a new person?

It took nine months to fully recover or regrow my adult energy. Even a walk around the block was too much. I kept returning to my memory of the dance and the healer's words, "A new blueprint is being laid down." I waited as a mother waits for a child.

That summer I had a dream. A young boy bought his father, his sister and me a beautiful house. But it was too expensive. The father felt suckered into this deal by his son, knowing he'd wind up responsible for it. Overwhelmed he took out a gun to shoot himself. I screamed. Instead he popped pills and caused great family dishonor. On top of this, the father was taken away to be the first witness in an enormous court case. It had to do with his son. We, the family, were separated. The devil showed up, worked the crowd and turned people toward less valuing ways. As I watched I heard a voice say, "We were in Islam."

It was the summer of 2001. Before this I had never thought of Islam. The events of 9/11 would occur three months later just as my energy returned to normal. At the time, the dream seemed odd. I couldn't attach personal meaning to the symbols. In retrospect however, I realized the son in the dream was George W. Bush. He was not only overextending his family, father, and ancestors, he was overextending his country, turning us to less valuing ways and bringing shame on us all.

My transformation prepared me for 9/11. I had firsthand experience that rebirth is possible and that a new blueprint was being laid down. I found myself chanting "Love is patient, Love is kind, Love is not jealous, or boastful. The greatest of these is Love." These words were not wishful thinking, but physics, the fundament of the biosphere. Love lays down a new blueprint.

Feeling such utter change in myself, I hoped that my somatic adventures would eliminate more of my obnoxious tendencies: my resistance to change, my dramatic nature, the resentments that piled up, and my worst fault of all, the undercurrent of anxiety and rage that I desperately wanted to hide. But, whatever physical transformation I had been through did not change my personality. To the contrary, I became less easy going at the same time that I loved more deeply.

The day President Bush declared war on Iraq I took thirteen lemons and a wad of black fabric to a class I taught on Dance and Social Action at Pacific School of Religion. Not knowing what I would do with them, they became props for a dance of lemon-tation. Wrapping myself in black, I declared to the class, "I will not refuse the dark anymore. No more wars with darkness, dark people, dark energy, difficult emotions, nighttime fears! I welcome the holy dark." The black fabric whipped around. The next thing I knew I was tossing lemons. They flew out to the class like small grenades of yellow hope until three remained. Creator, Son, and Holy Spirit flashed to mind. I squeezed them hard over my head, baptizing myself in their outrageous acidic juice. Bush, lemons, war. I made lament-aid and got sticky with it. Oddly lightened, the way that putting lemon on your hair in summer brings out highlights, grief turned to laughter. Laughter told the truth.

When the U.S. made its first strike against Iraq I wept at church and wrote "Forsaking Religion."

Today and for all days forward—
I protest American dreams of light
as long as Americans refuse infinite unlight
I protest six hundred sixty-six beliefs
if beliefs won't sing as a mother's love
I protest any god, goddess or ungod
whose name permits terror by human hands.
I protest religion, especially Christianity
as long as kill is any part of it.
See then my grief.
20 years ordained
protestant minister
I scorn my own faith.
Only protest remains.

The wedge between my inherited "tradition" and me grew. Faith remained. Courage to love? Having made the long trek across a bombed out plain of communal disaster, I knew what courage wasn't. Courage isn't a feeling. It's the ability to breathe when everything tells you to tighten and "Give up." Courage to love implies loving when you aren't loved. Why did I need to learn this? I listened for the voices to teach me.

Tradition sang a gold leafed song:
"Forgive us our trespasses
as we forgive those
that trespass
against us."

I ask, "How?"

Mother Wisdom sang:
"Be a body breathing,
willing to suffer a moment
instead of a million years.
Dance with despair,
without being swallowed by it.

Love past the compulsion
to fix everything."

Dancing Jesus piped in:
"Grace dances. Dance ye all.
Who does not dance?
Does not know what comes to pass.
Do you suffer?
Learn to suffer.
So as not to suffer."

An inaudible voice whispered:
"Dance, story, song, silence,
are the tributaries of your soul.
To retrieve power
dance, sing
tell the truth and be still."

7 | The Lucky Dark

> *Dance when you are broken open. Dance if you've*
> *torn the bandage off. Dance in the middle of the fight-*
> *ing. Dance and you're perfectly free.* —RUMI

I DON'T THINK DREAMS are only about the dreamer. I believe
that human consciousness is communal. Modern people have carried the benefits of individual freedom to such an extreme that we
have forgotten how much we are of one piece. I believe that we create for each other as well as ourselves. In the Bible Jacob won a seat
in the court of a foreign King for his ability to prophetically dream
and translate meaning to the powers that be. The only problem is
that, like art, dreams are subjective. We have to decide whether to
swallow these things whole or take them with a grain of salt.

The summer of 2002 I dreamt a world dream. More like art than
not, I put it into this poem.

> *Suited up against the dark nights,*
> *trying to find an answer for every howl*
> *and dance joy back from hell,*
> *suddenly, OUT OF NOWHERE*
> *I looked up.*
> *A rainbow stitched the night sky.*

Night rainbow? I checked my lenses,
elbowed my neighbor, "Did you see that?"
The stitch duplicated into multicolored
spherical, fractals of light,
each enwrapping an open space of
light born from infinite, unlit sources.
Rainbow eggs torrentially divided,
multiplied, hailed down.
Unprepared to run light-footed,
I wore high terrain boots, for hard work
and clodded toward the village square,
Many shoes were abandoned by the roadside.
I took off my boots and ran barefoot
into the aurora borealis flood that was
consuming and, swallowing the world.

Awake, I wondered, "Is this how it will happen? A future coming at us over which we have no control? Apocalyptic death? Apocalyptic hope?" Something enormously "other" is inherent in a miracle. Strike us dead or let us dance, I don't know how well we'll do it, but experience told me that bodies will alter and be offered up every time. A rainbow world is coming.

I had abandoned secret hopes of being any kind of religious prom princess or culturally creative up-and-comer. I still wrestled with the spidery web of forlorn conclusions and the promises of liberation from the very sources that suppressed it. What should a grown woman do with regret's hushed tears, hope lost, ideals lost, grace lost, love turned bitter? I was fatigued from the tyranny of not "making it" in institutions I'd vowed to save. I wanted badly to unstick from re-running, re-gretting, and being resent-fully yours. Should I once more re-work my inner architecture or merely say aloud this isn't what I want and nothing will bring it back. Why not be honest at least about regret?

Having flopped in "race relations" and that rare form, the theology school musical, I did what some confused people do, I signed up for doctoral work. A store-front university in Berkeley called the Western Institute of Social Research offered an intimate, multi-racial student body steeped in Pablo Friere's Pedagogy of the Oppressed. Interviewing to be admitted, I saw Fred Astaire and Ginger Rogers in a frame on the desk of the advisor, a sign.

As a student of "WISR" I quickly discovered that learning amongst people of color is a far cry from studying among well meaning white folk. My unconscious racism immediately surfaced when an African American guy added his two cents to a seminar. I observed myself think, "Are people of color really this smart?" I was shocked as I immediately recognized the smack of racism. Other thoughts that lurked backstage began promenading themselves in full view.

For years I had told myself that there were no people of color in my life. I began to sort out that actually, my white culture and white teachers were blotting out the presence and stories of friends with darker skin. I needed to take to heart the people of color in my life.

I dug out interracial memories—old Polaroids buried in my psychic drawers—and began redecorating the walls of my identity and imagination. Snapshots included:

- *"The Projects," Normont Elementary School Good Grooming Award.* Earl Paysinger and I compete for "Best Dressed" in Mr. Laney's class. Earl is African-American. So is Mr. Laney. I win one week. Earl wins the next.

- *Fleming Junior High, 8th grade hall monitor.* I watch as the Girls' Vice Principal says to Gail Stephens, "Get to class." Gail spits out sunflower seeds. The VP asks me, "What did she do?" I tell her. Gail is suspended and threatens to beat me up.

- *LA Airport.* Italian foreign exchange student Maria Teresa Tresorio comes to live with us for a year. I cry for joy. After two months of smoking, cussing, laundry hung around our room, and communist books, she moves to another family.

- *The Mountains.* Best friend Joanne Murakami joins our Methodist youth backpack camp. She'd never been to a Christian youth group and is moved by the kindness shown her.

- *Narbonne High School.* Mrs. Mac invites Lateesha and me to travel to Ensenada to perform on TV. I speak no Spanish but feel welcome in Baja California.

- *Great America.* Earl Paysinger is senior class president and I am vice president. We get to visit Great America as a graduation night location. On a log ride I sit in his lap, unsure how to relate.

- *Prom night on the Queen Mary.* I'm a prom princess standing with head cheerleader Cheryl Okomoto, blond Debra, and the Latina woman I don't really know. The Latina woman is crowned Queen.

- *UCLA dorm.* Roommate Naomi and I both like to sew, sing, hike, decorate, and laugh about our dads. Her dad is a devout Jew. Mine runs marathons with "Winton for Jesus" on his shirt.

- *Cruising Sunset Boulevard.* Tony Padilla takes me on a date in a low rider car. I feel weird, remembering high school jokes about "cruising down Lomas, in Tortilla Flats."

- *UCLA Dance Studio Concert.* I run lights. An African American classmate oils her skin and rolls on the floor in a dance about slavery. When told, "It makes the floor slippery for other dancers," she uses oil anyway. The audience applauds her piece, but I don't give her a second bow light. Later have to apologize.

- *UCLA Black Studies Department.* Dr. King, African Religions professor looks like Santa, pours libations to the ancestors, and gives away books he has written. He loves Africa.

- *Sierra Leone.* Forgetting it is taboo to photograph sacred moments, at a girls coming out ceremony, I snap picture camera. Black faces stare.

- *Los Gatos Synagogue office.* Rabbi Nahum Ward, after having come to InterPlay, shares an art Midrash process with me. As I meditate on Moses ascending Mt. Sinai, for the first time I grasp the importance of sacred boundaries.

- *San Jose Cathedral.* A mass in honor of the archangels. Dressed in white and black, Wing It! members Beth Hoch, a white woman, and David McCauley, a black man, dance a duet, stirring my soul.

- *Christian Church of Alameda.* Filipino families sit on one side of church and sing with gusto. I sit on the other side with aging white folks and try to keep up.

- *Consultant for a university staff retreat.* African-Americans fume about unfair pay while the visionary white leader shares his newest idea. A South American Indian board member suggests the leader attend to his present field before plowing new ones.

The more I looked, the more snapshots I found. Looking back at the ocean of diversity called life, I leaned toward middle class educated folks. Seminary, the church that ordained me, churches that hired art colleagues, my close friends and me were culturally similar. I had to consciously choose more color if I wanted it.

The walls of my house were beige. I wanted color, but never set aside cash, effort, or time to experiment with color until I got to Katharine's studio. She set everything up, encouraged you to go for it, and cleaned up afterward.

Katharine put not one or two, but three white canvases in front of me. She knows I think big. Like a kid on a high dive, I raised my brush and was surprised to plunge into the black paint. I blacked out all three sheets. Over that I layered on images. When the paint had dried there was a tree rooted in dark soil, its branches embracing sun and moon. The colors looked richer and truer with the dark behind them as I physically understood for the first time that the universe doesn't arise from a white canvas. Creation emerges from inky black.

Howard Thurman, twentieth century African American mystic, began his book, *The Luminous Darkness: A Personal Interpretation of the Anatomy of Segregation and the Ground of Hope*, by quoting a deep-sea diver.

> *"Enroute to the floor of the ocean the diver first passes through the 'belt of the fishes.' This is a wide band of light reflected from the surface of the sea. From this area he moves to a depth of water that cannot be penetrated by light above the surface. It is dark, foreboding, and eerie. The diver's immediate reaction is apt to be one of fear and sometimes one of a sudden spasm of panic that soon passes. As he drops deeper and deeper into the abyss, slowly his eyes begin to pick up the luminous quality of the darkness; what was fear is relaxed and he moves into the lower region with confidence and peculiar vision."*

Thurman added an additional line from Psalm 139. "If I say, surely the darkness shall cover me, even the night shall be light about me...The darkness and the light are both alike to thee."

What is the color of hope? Perhaps freedom begins with the darkest of all colors. Is that why Wing It! wears black to perform? It's the easiest color to unify. Plus it made us look thinner. Black is not only beautiful it's mysterious and foundational.

The more I got mixed up with color and coloring, the more my affinity with whiteness lost hold. People of color began befriending me in magical, effortless ways. Like finger painting, coloring led me outside my cultural lines to a bigger landscape. Color itself was a transformative agent.

Phil already knew about all this. Sitting over in his corner he's forever quietly painting, hand dying, crocheting, and drawing in every imaginable color possible. A color fiend, never content with one or two colors, he picked eleven colors for our InterPlay office walls. Beyond that Phil wrote in his book, *The Slightly Mad Rantings of a Body Intellectual Part One*,

Black, white, red, yellow, brown. Who ever thought up that system? Obviously not a gay man. Here is a new system for dividing people according to skin color: mocha, butternut, beige, cinnamon, midnight, ecru, ebony, cream, taupe, coffee, rose, parchment, melon, ochre, seashell, terra cotta, olive, ginger, taro, beech-wood, tan, bone, sandstone, caramel, golden, peach, cloud, oak, burnt umber. OK—everybody get organized! Into your groups!

Black history month at Sumpter County Elementary near Americus, Georgia, doesn't fit into a snapshot. It was my first experience of teaching in the South. Kids carted a gargantuan Black History book offstage to made room for me and Phil to dance and sing songs like "A body is a body is a body is a body" written for kids in Katie's third grade class

Big body, bitty body, girly curly burly Yes!
a body is a body is a body is a body...

ripe body

green body

peach
brown
purple, YES!
a body is a body is a body is a body.
Grace body, gristle body, airy, dirty, slushy, YES!
a body is a body is a body is a body.
Wise body, wild body, sneezing, snoring, burping, YES!
a body is a body is a body is a body.
Holy body, hungry body, dancing, feasting, a-la, YES!
a body is a body is a body is a body.

Heat body, blizzard body, forest, ocean, city, YES!
a body is a body is a body is a body.
bony body, flabby body, muscly, hairy, toothy, YES!
a body is a body is a body is a body.
Show body, nobody, flirty, wordy, nerdy, YES!
a body is a body is a body is a body.
Well body, sick body, struggle, huggle, cuddle, YES!
a body is a body is a body is a body.
Whole body, soul body, quirky, perky, kooky YES!
a body is a body is a body is a body.
Sleepy body, sheepy body, cozy, toesy, dozy, YES!
a body is a body is a body is a body.
Your body, my body, just the way we are, YES!
a body is a body is a body is a body.

In front of four hundred children at a time, I gleefully lifted the white principal off his feet and talked to kids about power and leverage. Duty-heavy teachers crossed their arms. Children were eager to shake off their leechy pain, go crazy, and be free.

Walking the halls, I read the writing on the wall. On green-lined school paper taped to the walls, elementary children praised black heroes in their cursive truths, saying things like, "Hero, without you, whites would take over the world."

What was I doing here? Debra Weir, former Wing It! member, moved to Americus with her husband who'd been transferred to the headquarters of Habitat for Humanity. Debra wanted to bring InterPlay to the schools.

In Americus a trembling thing grew from generation to generation, a kudzu so thick and heavy that only warriors could cut it and still look you in the eye. On one end of town President Carter was born. On the other end, thirteen thousand union soldiers had been imprisoned, died, and were buried by Confederate soldiers. Between these poles former slaves and slave owners had become global villagers building habitats of shelter for the homeless.

That night laying in bed I thought I heard a black ghost say, "Don't love me. Love only breathes air on a pain so big it can't find home."

Then I dreamt a nightmare. A lawsuit was brought against me by five kind, but determined African Americans. "Someone must pay," they said. Although I was changing heart and mind and walking toward the light, it wasn't enough. The suit was against the historical privileges of not responding, not knowing, not changing sooner, thereby crippling others over and over with endless hit and run refusals to take responsibility for crimes committed.

When I awoke I knew then that, until perpetrators recognize, apologize, and forgive themselves, no one walks away free. I couldn't forgive myself. So I scribed a prayer, "I'm too little for pain so big and don't know how I'm to sing here. Nothing but shadow to this dark, Angels, bend your wings; shield the people of the velvet dark from vacuous white eyes. Carry us all over our anguish into a more promising land."

Masankho Banda walked through the door of the Pacific School of Religion classroom and beamed at me. He wanted to meet the woman who taught dance and religion. As soon as I saw him I called him Grace-man even before I knew his story. He'd fled Malawi, Africa, when his father, Aleke Banda, was imprisoned for contesting the president and fighting for the Malawi constitution. Through Amnesty International Masankho escaped to a college in Ohio, and gradually became the peacemaker he is, using song, dance, and storytelling to give rise to life and connection. His grandmother in Tukumbo, Malawi, watched him dance as a young child and said, "Masankho, when you grow up you will make people happy through song and dance." He combined his father's political will with his insistence on the arts as vehicles for peace.

Masankho joined Wing It!, became an InterPlay leader, and a beloved colleague. He and I both lived far from our family origins but believed that ancestors still guided us, lifted us, and caused us to stumble when we were foolish. Even though I couldn't tell you who my grandparents are, I intuitively agreed with Masankho when he said, "The largest group of unemployed is our ancestors." Modern people seemed to use machetes on their own tree, giving no thought to hacking at the roots of family wisdom. Some treated their families as dead wood. Were we a nation of walking stumps? Is deforesting the planet parallel to our treatment of ancestral lines.

A New Zealander told Masankho and me that Maori people see ancestry as a fountain. Descendants ride it at the top. The Maori warn that those who make decisions far from their family tree, who forget the stories of grandparents, and don't connect to the dead, often find their life force diminished. They have only governments and employers for accountability; institutions that can cut you off in a minute.

Sitting on my own stump, I meditated on fragments of family history: the jail time, alcoholism, gambling, "unwanted pregnancies," domestic violence, and endless immigrations, some of us arriving when America was a "new world," others coming in the 1900s. I knew little of ordinary or good times.

In my thoughts I tended my stump and honored its limits. Finding a rotting stump on the street, I dragged it home and used it as an altar. I confessed the role of my people in collective misconduct and grieved the ways we were not able to stand up to forces that cut us down. I clung to the promises of the prophet Isaiah who sang, "You shall be like a watered garden, like a spring of water whose waters never fail. Your ancient ruins shall be rebuilt; you shall raise up the foundations of many generations and be called the repairer of the breach, the restorer of streets to live in" (Isaiah 58:11-12).

Masankho and I began using dance, drum, and imagination to travel into the intuitive caverns of memory. When he danced on behalf of my ancestors he found a few women who just wanted the best for my lifework and me. They gave him the message, "You are not required to heal the past. Go on." They helped me surrender the burden of healing generational shame.

Without knowing anything of my prayers, my mother's companion, George, a devout agnostic, began to research my mother's family tree. George quietly pulled up and documented Wentworth family roots extending back through laundry workers, laborers, mayors, pioneers, early governors and across the ocean all the way back to

England's Magna Carta and the largest castle in England, the Wentworth castle. With his aid, I reunited my story with Wentworths, Wintons, Stumpfs, Hugs, Mossmans, and many others. The stump was no longer a stump. Like the stump of Jesse, it burst with green shoots. When you can say that your lineage extends as far back as people can remember, you stand taller.

8 | *Purification*

Time's bitter flood will rise
Your beauty perish and be lost
For all eyes but these eyes."

—WILLIAM BUTLER YEATS

THE TURN OF THE MILLENNIUM WAS NO JOYRIDE. Mayan, Hopi, and Christian apocalpyticists forecast the end times. I looked around. The world was at war. No one called it a world war, but the World Wide Web, intercontinental evacuations and immigrations, air travel and world trade connected everyone. A war in one place affected everyone. In a letter I begged President Bush to stop his war on the Middle East. "Conquest begets slavery. I won't stand among the privileged that pretend that conquests heal. I'd rather sacrifice money, heat, and cars. Consumer of a 'good life,' I'd rather choose simplicity, (ask me to do this!) rather than beleaguer my daughter's century with the irreversible, exhausting tolls of war. Violence never victors. Only unconditional neutral regard leads to the foundational way of the universe. I pray for the day we choose this path. I pray for Iraq and all our enemies. In the end, the Bible says, 'The leaves of the Tree of Life are for the healing of the nations.' War is our most meager attempt at Life. Shake the Tree. Try another way."

Amidst this, the needs of my family and work escalated. Friends were tsunamied by divorce, cancer, suicide, death of parents, loss of

185

jobs, and threats of homelessness. Astrologers were having a field day. Mercury, Mars, Jupiter, whatever planet it was, wreaked havoc just as my daughter hit puberty and Stephen and I decided to drive our psychic planes into the twin towers of our marriage. Old patterns had to fall. Behaviors had to change. We went to family therapy, individual therapy, and special meetings with nothing but faith, knowing it was too late to turn back. Between panic attacks, helpless tears, clouded thoughts, and occasional lucid moments, a voice reassured me that all this would pass. I danced and breathed to keep the storms moving.

One day while cleaning house, the book *Descent to the Goddess: A Way of Initiation for Women* fell off the shelf. I opened it and read about Innana, the goddess who descended through seven gates into the underworld to meet her sister. At each gate she had to discard jewels and clothes until naked, she greeted her sister, the dark goddess who immediately impaled her on a peg. Over three days Innana turned into rotting, green meat until her dancing spirit friends snuck down, rescued her, and carried her back to the surface. Once again, dancers were the way out!

The myth of Innana confronted all my illusions of the "good daughter," the socially adapted, competent, female of society. Innana couldn't match her sister's darker powers and the dark goddess stuck it to her in an inevitable initiation that crucified her beauty and social naiveté.

In my case, the dark goddess took my soul in her hands and dared me to do the same. If I didn't she threatened to keep it. The only good news was that dancing spirits were the ticket out. During my marital and parenting descent, my fear felt atomic. I tried to squeeze it, hold it, and make it smaller than my psyche. None of this worked. So, instead I offered the dark goddess the honor she was due and hyperventilated.

The dark goddess awoke parts of me I rejected: the uncaring, poisonous, foul voice that says, "I don't give a rat's ass." I grew intimate with the finalizing, ultimate, objectifying, dead honest, unflinching, eyeball piercing, overly-rational me. Down in the chaotic underworld of truth where the myths of the feminine are shattered, the divine feminine pegged me and marked me as inescapably human. I had to learn that Love isn't a security pact to bypass pain. It's bigger than that.

꙰

I dreamt that my pickup truck was stuck on an ice bridge when a thaw came. I asked a bystander, "Go, run, and get a rope to pull the truck off the precipice." A warrior woman jumped into the driver's seat. To save the truck she sacrificed herself to the engine. It ate her alive. She didn't cry. In a trance of pain she muttered something about its intensity. I thought, "How stupid! All I wanted was to back the pickup off the ice."

To keep images of peace alive the keepers of imagination navigate fear daily. Each day this seemed harder. I observed sensitive bodies complain more of anxiety. Mystics worked harder. InterPlayers danced on behalf of collective helplessness. Dot com crashes gave way to soldiers who made hasty wedding vows before going off to war. Alice Walker was arrested on the White House steps. When a writer tears herself away from her solitary craft you know it is a dangerous day. Leaders trying to figure out how to transform health care, politics, and our eco-less egos hit the wall. Books written on happiness were becoming bestsellers. Unable to find helpful news on the television, it was graffitied on walls, "There can be no security without peace, there can be no peace without freedom, there can be no freedom without justice, and there can be no justice without love."

Coleman Barks, the Rumi translator, spoke at the National Cathedral in Washington, D.C., and exposed the utter lack of imagination inherent in male political thinking by offering alternatives to the President's war in Iraq.

> *Medical services, transportation inside Iraq, lots of big colorful buses—let the pilgrims paint them!—along with many other ideas that will be thought of later during the course of this innocently, blatantly foolish project will all also be funded by the U.S. government. There's*

> *a practice known as sama, a deep listening to poetry and music, with sometimes movement involved. We could experiment with whole nights of that, staying up until dawn, sleeping in tents during the day. So, instead of war, there's a peace period.... I'll be the first to volunteer for two weeks of wandering winter deserts and reading Hallaj, Abdul Qadir Gilani, dear Rabia, and the life-saving* 1001 Arabian Nights.

The dance of life had a bigger role to play than ever before. Everyone from psychic children to the African American activist bell hooks confirmed that all strategies pile up in a heap without love. If my forty plus years had taught me anything, it was that love is an embodiment that can't be broken down into an act, idea, or plan. Only by dancing our brutal, tender life do we arrive at the lovemaking essential to living together in diverse community. *Only the literal dance of life can help us transcend our wounds and heal our borders. Play is the opposite of war and creativity is the opposite of strife.*

Remembering the dream of the apocalyptic rainbow spheres descending like planetary vitamins, I knew that a homeopathic remedy like dance, play, and telling our stories was crucial. InterPlayers discover that the sooner we get to deep play the sooner we stabilize. Even Phil and I moved through intense friction and recovered our interpersonal health by dancing hand to hand. In the gentling of a dance we could not remain antagonistic. We calmed down. Love won.

I tuned into new prophets who spoke of "Another Way." Arundhati Roy said, "Another world is not only possible, she is on her way. And on a quiet day...you can hear her breathing." Henri Nouen had said, "The world is waiting for new saints, ecstatic men and women who are so deeply rooted in the love of God that they are free to imagine a new international order." Theodore Roetke said, "What we need is more people who specialize in the impossible."

Even those less grandiose pointed the way, like Anne Lamott who wrote, "This is the most profound spiritual truth I know: that even when we're most sure that love can't conquer all, it seems to anyway." And, Deena Metzger said, "There are those who are trying to set fire to the world, we are in danger, there is time only to work slowly, there is no time not to love." Duke Ellington, too humbly said, "I merely took the energy it takes to pout and wrote some blues."

※

One question plagued me. "How could I ask for peace in the US when in my little family of three I struggled so hard to achieve it?" I didn't lash out with fists or weapons at my family, but those close to me felt my anger as a threat. I was prone to judgmental reactionary hissy fits. As a "loving person" I worked hard to disguise my little miss smarty pants. At least I'd committed to disarm.

I sat on a worn-out sofa at WISR, the storefront university, with my advisor when I finally confessed my judgments of the other students sitting around the seminar tables. I judged them as I had my seminary colleagues. The embarrassing confession outed my unspoken resistance to intellectualism that created obstacles to the profound teachings of body wisdom. I knew thinking to be a multidimensional, creative, embodied act and yet this felt iconoclastic in academia. I waltzed around with a chip on my shoulder in spite of the fact that the multicultural WISR faculty had taught me that action research is a valid academic methodology and my advisor, an anthropologist, emphasized the subjective nature of all human information. She embraced interviewing people, life, and myself to test and revise my theories.

As I spoke with her, struggling to shift my resistant posture, I suddenly realized that I was judging myself as one who merely "danced around." Based on the western academic model I had an inferiority complex about thinking. All of a sudden, like shedding armor that had grown too tight, I dropped my resistance to the intellect. I claimed my place. I love to think. I think like everybody else. I am an intellectual. Even more, I am a full-fledged member of the conspiratorial academy of theology and street dancing. I had no need to apologize, no need to feel badly that I don't have a Ph.D. If anything, I am more like an academic than not. I think a lot, talk a lot, write a lot, and use up a lot of time musing.

Shortly afterwards, I left WISR without certification. Both humbled and smarter, instead of paying for a PhD, I bought my daughter braces.

> *I am all words*
> *words running everywhere*
> *on and on*
> *i do not shut up*
> *but add to the flood.*
> *i build a little boat*
> *diving into language*
> *as if it mattered.*

❈

My mother didn't laugh when I joked that I'd spent my retirement money on my youth. Still, getting older has perks. Establishing oneself is one of them. The InterPlay dream was slowly paying off. Miraculously and intentionally, Phil and I received paychecks. With the support of community we bought a derelict downtown Oakland building and made it into a sacred center of creativity, community, and change called InterPlayce. The InterPlay system spread. We moved from being founders of InterPlay to managing its home office.

Approaching age fifty, seeking a nest for my husband, daughter, and dog Christopher (also known as Yogadogananda for his capacity to stretch backward), Stephen and I investigated creative strategies for home co-ownership with friends. All of them fell through. My best friend and neighbor, Beth, mustered up a sizeable down payment and bought a 1960's condo five blocks away. I secretly whined. Jealous, I walked Christopher down the street to a small pier by the Elsie Rhommer Bird Sanctuary overlooking the San Francisco Bay. I prayed a bold prayer. I needed a secure home. It needn't be big. I just needed a view of nature.

The next day Beth called. There was a condo for sale where she lived with a view overlooking a lagoon and the East Bay hills. It was perfect. In three weeks escrow closed. We moved in on Halloween.

Beth and I, neighbors again, joked about the InterPlay ghetto at Laguna Hacienda.

The inconveniences of condo life were blessings to me. I felt smug about curbing consumerism. It was harder for our teenager to avoid us. Stephen and I weren't responsible for major maintenance. Laundry that formerly heaped up in piles got washed and folded in the common laundry room. The dog had to be walked along the scenic shoreline where we picked up his poop instead of stepping in it in the backyard. My home was no longer a stopover for everyone, which translated into more rest in relation to my husband. From our deck, ducks, geese, egrets, pelicans, and great blue herons rested during their migratory paths. Wings. Flight. Home.

9 | End Times

Last night
God posted
on the tavern wall
a decree for all of love's inmates
which read:
If your heart cannot find a joyful work
The jaws of this world
will probably
grab hold of your
sweet ass.
—HAFIZ

HURRICANE KATRINA HEADED FOR NEW ORLEANS as I flew across the country with a TV screen fixed to the seat in front of me. From close up and high above, I watched Katrina brew, tensions mount, and horrendous waves violate the shore. I watched people flee and find protection. I saw strangely quiet lines of people enter a sports dome that looked more like a Titanic than an Ark. Sensitized to the South, I witnessed nature aim at the center of the African-American art world, threatening to obliterate Soul itself. When weather forecasters said, "We've never seen a storm like this," I took it personally, pleading, "It's not fair!"

The whips of Katrina slammed New Orleans and my frustrations at both church and state about the Iraq war, poverty, race, and anti-Semitism welled up. The born-again president who waged a world-wide war on terrorists acted lame in the wake of black people who cried for help from the rooftops of their flooded homes. Dancing wasn't enough for this level of disaster. Writing wasn't enough to dispel my fury and despair. Our country's leaders fumbled. Didn't they know that this was more than a storm? Scar tissue from slavery and the unhealed gash of the war between the North and the South lay exposed as the President flew back from vacation and "looked down" on the disaster zone. Even newscasters, standing amidst people waiting in sewage, broke from their neutral stances in outrage. Weren't elected officials aware of African-Americans' distrust in governmental response? Was this ignorance or choice? Did America have no boat big enough to rescue its yanked, swamped, shaking people? Why was there no one to empathetically speak of our sorrow or overwhelm?

A dark-eyed refugee said of the President, "That man irritates me down to my skinny bones." She knew a white face and a speech were no sign of relief.

That Sunday at church there was a similar delay of emotional response. My religious community was respected for progressive values. We affirmed gay ordination and marriage. After 9/11 a minister immediately built liaisons with the local Islamic center. But, the Sunday after the hurricane, my vibrating grief heard only one prayer made for the victims. My heart sank. On TV, people of color rushed aid across the racial divide and ferried the hurricane refugees to the East Oakland mall, one of the poorest areas in the Bay Area's black community. But, my predominately white church was almost mute.

I snapped. I could not hold my seat. I stormed out. During an era marked by an unjust war, religious conservatism, and racial imbalance, the temperature at church felt intolerably tepid. Friends in the gay rights movement had said that the silence of liberal Christians is harder to bear than that of those who are openly hateful. Silence is compliance. Holocaust survivors say this too. I couldn't stand the silence in the face of our history of abuses. My personal acquaintance with abuse wouldn't let me "just hang in there."

I ranted at my computer. "Ten thousand litanies kill the soul! TV underscores violence with more words and I ONLY WANT TO GRIEVE. After that I want to ACT. Would we blather on at a deathbed?"

I heard an African-American church leader diagnose the white church's lack of emotion as a disease of the body. Why was "decent and in order" carved over the door of euro-centric sanctuaries? What did we know about the danger of rage? Had we beheaded emotion in hopes of creating a new world?

George Lakoff, who analyzed the differences between progressive and conservative religious worldviews and their effect on politics in his best-selling book *Don't Think of an Elephant*, said that progressives are guided by two values: empathy and responsibility. Where was our empathy? Were we "free" to be quiet, reserved, and thoughtful? Has security lifted us above anguish? Is rational thinking really our salvation? If we don't move together, would we ever feel together? I saw the pulpit, the organ, the lack of democratic, spontaneous movement and emotion, the lack of rituals for shame, anger, rage, grief, love, affection and real joy and felt a tidal wave of intolerance rise up in the ground of my being. How could this be? Only recently had I wept to join this people. I loved and trusted the leaders. I was never personally cursed here. On the contrary I had received comfort among this congregation.

In a documentary *Searching for the Wrong Eyed Jesus*, white poor people in the South sing songs thick with the raw texture of prison, Saturday night dancing and drinking, and Sunday morning Pentecostalism. They exform and heal themselves on a body level, having little other choice. On the other hand, affluent "liberal" people are embarrassed to cry in public, not to mention a social no-no like breathing out loud. Our shame comes easily. Western worship seems to reinforce this. I was suddenly sick of it.

> *Sick of wordy songs*
> *sick of Jesus stories*
> *recited 5000 times*
> *Sick of sermons*
> *Sick of hymns preserving*
> *a rotting romance with history*
> *Sick of "good liturgy" that*
> *deals out Caesar over and over*
> *Sick of beheadings*
> *Indian, Black, Asian, and Iraqi.*

at the hands of "Christians"
who steer our ships across seas
of demon-cratic invasions
Sick of myself.
How will I keep from
standing up in this whore-ship
and screaming?

Two weeks after Hurricane Katrina at an InterPlayce presentation on diverse ways to embody ritual, the presenter offered an apologetic. Her presentation was based in the Christian tradition. We'd be singing Christian standard hymns like "Praise to the Lord, the Almighty, The King of Creation" and "The Churches one foundation is Jesus Christ her Lord," I looked around the InterPlayce and saw close Jewish friends. As we began to sing, the exclusive "Lord" language" stood up on its hind legs. I stopped. Then I asked, "If I couldn't sing these songs in the presence of friends at InterPlayce, why did I sing them at church?

The presenter invited Wing It! to dance. I took my place. Rage flashed. Off balance, I pulled the muscle behind my right knee. If my legs are pillars of righteousness, the right one was knocked out from under me. Months later after the injury hadn't healed I went to a kinesiologist. Working on my knee like a shaman he asked if the injury could have to do with transforming anger in relationship to others. Me, angry?

I made a new covenant. I would not speak of Jesus in any way that diminished other people or their faith. In the multidimensional global house of love, like the innkeeper in Bethlehem, I had no room for a single entry god, even a tiny baby God. I would build no more altars to singularities. No G no O no D, no one story, no one image, no one person. No one name, nation, or church, no United Way with everyone marching to one rhythm, sleeping peacefully with one savior in one manger. I would only honor a thousand different teachings and pray for the faith to fall backwards into the mighty arms of life. I started fasting from the words "savior, lord, messiah." This made singing Christmas carols and going to church dicey.

On World Communion Sunday, sitting in the church's newly remodeled sanctuary made accessible to wheelchairs and large performance groups, I should have been glad. Mentally preparing for a United Nations 60th anniversary performance focusing on eight goals, the first of which is to eradicate poverty by 2015, I looked up at the chancel. The gaping holes for the soon-to-be installed million-dollar organ stared back. The chasm between the church's prosperity and the world's need was in my face. Crisis after crisis, tsunami and hurricane, and the daily poverty outside of InterPlayce in Oakland grew more intense everyday.

As an artist I embraced extravagance. I believe the poor need cathedrals, as much if not more than the wealthy. I loved Mary Magdalene for taking expensive nard and pouring it over Jesus' feet. When the disciples asked Jesus, "Why did you let her do that? What about the poor?" He answered, "The poor you always have with you. But you only have me for awhile." But a million dollar organ installed in the face of the Katrina aftermath? Could we at least be like the disciples and question the weird contradiction of hurricane survivors scattered homeless across America and an entire city lying in ruins as we applauded our multi-million dollar remodeled sanctuary and organ.

Constantly appalled at feeling orange red fury and eyes in the back of my head that spun around like someone with demon possession, I tried to find reasons for my reactions. I hadn't given up on reason. Had the devastation of the storm triggered memories of poverty? My family had no land or inheritance for generations. The Great Depression was never discussed. Too painful. Like my grandfathers I addictively looked for "easy street" while my grandmothers labored as laundrywomen and clerks. When Dad became an engineer, he purchased a tri-level house and furnished it in early swap meet. After my first year of college when Mom and Dad separated they said flat out, "You're on your own." The middle class I was in sat right next to the dump.

I approached my breaking point. The more that InterPlay and the dance of life sustained me, the more religion did not. Receiving a summons to attend a mandatory "Clergy Sexual Misconduct" workshop that was required to keep one's official standing as an ordained minister, my question was, "did I want to keep on standing like this?" Unhealed anguish about the three disastrous church ministries and the absence of church support for InterPlay had eaten away at my affiliation. I'd asked a regional minister to come to InterPlay to see my work and he said, "I don't have time. Too many churches in crisis."

Mustering the last vestiges of duty and hope, I went to the workshop, happily thrilled to see many old friends. Among them were the first ordained women clergy and gay clergy in our region. We embraced, laughed, and sat down together. When the presentation began we were shown a film about a predatory male pastor. Like the threats about Homeland Security, this was our red alert. This was no conversation about healthy sexuality or typical forms of sexual wandering. No acknowledgement that women clergy might offer a completely different perspective to sexual misconduct in the church. Instead, the leader chided us for lacking insurance against sexual misconduct, informed us that he worked in the insurance industry, and gave a call for insurance as the final altar call. Money! Sex! Fear! Again, I leapt up and stormed out. My ecclesiastical feet flew out from under me on my way out the door.

Rage grew. If I turned my attention to it, it shot up like a hot river. I felt complicit with historical patterns. Should I forgive tradition and move on? I didn't want to break covenant with my Christian community. They were the family that guided me, sheltered me, and showed me love. Neither did I want to dump more rage on the world.

I was desperate to shake it out. I could barely talk to anyone. Once again, I turned to art. I glued a rusty toy gun to an old family Bible and pasted an anonymous ransom note inside that said, "If a teaching does not make us more loving it should be put down." I collaged a card deck of one thousand cards with goddess images to balance out a preponderance of male images for God. I sent hate mail to God. "I hate a mainline church standing lame like an old woman struggling to remain dignified as her wardrobe reeks of urine. I hate the Righteous Christian Conspiracy's monotheistic belly curdling with self-serving, saying Victory! Master! Lord! Sovereign! I hate LORD religions that empty garbage everywhere calling it mercy. I hate that BIG FAT BOY GOD bloated in a stew made by overly educated babysitters."

What was wrong with me? I was the only white woman storming out of rooms and dancing up and down with rage. I was fine if I thought about anything but church or if I focused on InterPlay. But when I turned toward my faith tradition the fire came up. I was beginning to understand why some people couldn't tolerate joining the nice people at church. I had bodily compassion for African Americans who couldn't tolerate working with the white community one more day.

Then I had a holy tantrum. At a seminary chapel on World Aids day, Wing it! focused on African children with AIDS. We danced with children's empty clothes, no longer worn, no longer playing on swings and in the dirt. I stepped before the altar to dance and it happened. Mother Rage took over. I began stomping and exhorting. I was literally hopping mad.

A week later at a meeting to evaluate the chapel service I asked for feedback about breaking the rage barrier and an inner city African-American minister said under her breath, "We do rage at our church."

"SEE! People of color rage together!" I blurted. I left the meeting embarrassed, once again too strong, too aware, and too helpless.

That night I dreamt that a white snake came out of my mouth. Out of the throat of the white snake came a red flower. As the snake began to exit, it shit in my mouth. To hide my shame I swallowed the snake. The white snake came up again. Researching the images, I learned that in numerous cultures the white snake is a rare symbol of the uneasy power of the goddess. And public defecation? That's the most humiliating of all human acts. Defecating in one's own mouth? Oral Shame.

Rage and shame are inseparable partners. One necessitates the other. As rage moves our cry of truth out, shame retracts us for protection. Rage is born of powerlessness, culpability, and frustration. It anguishes over the very thing that is most vulnerable: our hurt. Shame prevents us from making ourselves any more vulnerable.

On the deadline to sign the ministerial standing form, I waited for a voice to tell me what to do. There were no voices to be heard. I didn't sign the paper. Instead of gaining relief, my rage intensified. Like the old hymn, "Oh, Love, that wilt not let me go," rage seemed to be love's other name. Rage wouldn't let me go. Either the prophet Jeremiah wanted me for his laughingstock sister or the dark goddess got the better of me. At a Wing It! retreat I got up to dance, and fell on my knees, yelling at God. Phil came onto the floor thrusting and dancing on my behalf. Penny Mann, an activist and retired minister, joined him. Finally, relief! Two strong bodies mirrored my struggle. The church, academia, or a therapist would have asked me to sit down, write, or analyze my experience. My emotional bottom line moved when I was heard artist to artist.

Their dance gave me courage to go forward. That and Ruth King, author of *Healing Rage: Women Transforming Rage into Peace* whose lifework focused on celebrating rage. In the quiet of her home I took a deep breath and laid out my predicament.

"Ruth! I've been enraged for one hundred straight days! I'm dangerously close to overthrowing temple furniture, insurance booths, oil vendors, and legalists whose ideologies control the heart."

With the warmth of motherhood and the stillness of Buddha, Ruth replied with a question that I will never forget, "Cynthia, how will you dignify your rage? How will you speak what you know?"

That was when I knew what I must do. I needed to protest. I needed to move the rage. I had to do something constructive with it.

First, I had to give it its due. Since my rage wasn't going away I developed my theory of emotion as weather systems. If a storm comes up we don't say, "It shouldn't rain." Emotion is our own involuntary ever-changing weather. We can predict low and high pressure systems, but the most common cultural joke is to laugh at the weather forecaster. Yet, we still tune into the weather because weather matters. Rage comes around, but it never stays. And that is OK.

Since my imagination seemed to need a rumpus room, I invented rules of fair play for dancing with rage.

1. You can put your feet in the river of rage if you can pull them out and put them in some other river. Don't get stuck in your rage river.

2. Use art, containers, altars, or platforms for rage.

3. Dignify rage, don't make it a problem.

4. Connect rage to love, humility, and self-respect.

5. Feed joy. Rage without joy can't inspire change.

6. Reassure the enraged. Dance on behalf of them.

7. Remember rage isn't absolute, even if it elevates itself over other emotions.

8. Come back to your little body if you lose yourself to big injustices.

9. Be gentle with sister shame.

10. Breathe, Breathe, Breathe.

11. Don't presume someone else's neutrality lacks the clarity of rage.

12. Claim and aim for what you want: Freedom.

My wants were probably too bold for my own good.

I WANT action and dreams that shake the bones
the rare crystal word that acts on us
songs that comfort mourners and
a drum that says we are alive, we are alive.

I WANT to dance white snakes and red streamers
around the white house.
to be a tree oracle appearing outside a lecture hall
dressed in sublime unmistakable treeness.

I WANT to rend robe and stole,
pass out chocolate kisses to street people.
build shrines to grief on city streets,
make garbage lands beautiful.
and InterPlay with neighbor, stranger, and land.

How would I dignify my rage? I wanted to renounce my ordination. At minimum, I wanted to get my spiritual alignment in right relation, to have the dance of life at the very center of my vow with Love.

I met with the regional head of my denomination and said what I could in thirty minutes. Although I secretly hoped that something would happen to intervene, I said "I want to renounce my ordination."

"Cynthia, why not keep your ordination, but let go of your standing?" he asked, referring to my active clerical relationship with the church.

Standing? Was I about to fall? The truth was InterPlay had spoiled me. If the dance of life and Christ hadn't led me toward InterPlay I might still be a minister. Standing? I had fallen to my knees a dozen times before the endless love of God. Maybe the problem was that my call wasn't born from standing.

In *Clergywomen: An Uphill Calling*, Barbara Brown Zikmund said "Clergywomen have a much broader view of ordination and the ways in which their ordination can be lived out in full-time ministry. Yet, one of the major reasons women are leaving local church ministry is the lack of support."

I said again, "No, I want to renounce my ordination."

He didn't flinch. He suggested that I meet with the Recognition and Standing Committee.

It was too complicated—all the history, the feminism, the sexual revolution, the fallout from the sixties, forces way beyond me. Things like word idolatry, racial apathy, suspicion of mysticism and repression of the body made it hard to dance. My concerns were so complex I decided to make a list. Thirteen "deals" pushed their way to the surface along with a list of corresponding body wisdom practices that I gathered in InterPlay. (See the appendix for the lists.)

There's no map through religious divorce. A few unruly Protestant disciples may get kicked out of their faith communities these days, but most just get bummed out and leave. I would have to ask my denomination to consciously release me from my vows. To do this I chose the same procedures required of me upon entering the ordination process. I spoke of my intention with friends, family, people at the seminary, and the recognition and standing committee. Then I wrote a paper and set up a meeting.

Charlotte was the first minister I told. I cried as I confessed that I had lost faith in mainstream Christianity. I had lost faith that my church would ever truly value the dance of life as a primary form of healing and spirituality. I mourned that as a dancer in church, ultimately I felt like a fly on a horse. A fly can cause the swish of a tail, but a horse needn't move for a fly or two. The dance and all that came with it was spiritually necessary to me, but not to the church. The church was like a person who doesn't exercise. Occasional attempts to exercise the collective body of faith were too little too late. As soon as it dances it is breathless and must sit down.

Charlotte asked me, "How did all this happen?"

I shared how Katrina had knocked me off my church feet. Racism had grown into a thorn in my flesh. I was seeing the larger unconscious practices that were oppressive. They had electrified my rage circuitry.

"Are you leaving the church?" she asked.

I had no plans to start a church or find a better one. I connect to the life and teachings of Jesus and value how Christian community cares for its members. The church is my family of origin, but not my destination. I was shedding a religious skin.

As we ended, Charlotte asked, "What can we do?"

Shrugging, I said in weariness, "Progressive churches with health and resources should commit to unlearn racism."

She said, "I accept."

It wasn't what I expected. We grasped hands in tears.

I distinctly felt a bat bite my foot. It was a dream but it felt so real I woke up. Pay attention, I thought. The workshop that day was in an Australian Anglican church that physically resembled the one that Stephen and I had co-pastored. People gathered. Half were new to InterPlay, including a bestselling journalist who'd retired, irreparably depleted by fighting the conservative tides. Others were ministers and activists. We moved, babbled, and got acquainted. I proposed we play with something they cared about, the refugees who were being refused entry to Australia. We would dance on their behalf.

I put on the CD player music sung by Australian refugees. The room flooded with emotion. A clergywoman stood paralyzed. A high school teacher curled up in a fetal position. Faces of activists pinched with anguish. The journalist fell off her center. Only the woman fresh out of the psych ward brightened to the upbeat music of refugees singing, "We belong! We belong!" I'd led the workshop into a pit of unprocessed emotion.

A heard an echo, "Pay attention!"

Around the dinner table that night the journalist fired off her breathless, angry, deconstructions. At the same time InterPlay activists laughed and tossed a birthday scarf from person to person inviting each other to tell a story of change. Whenever the conversation got stuck in whiny complaint an InterPlayer blurted, "I have a story!"

Emma Goldman quipped, "If I can't dance I don't want to be part of your revolution." Those who protest can easily become the same dour, rigid, angry oppressor that they fight. As I watched the drama at the table, I felt the sting of the bat. The journalist's rage had gone too far. Spiritually anorexic, unbeautied in a baggy t-shirt and jeans, her hair, arms, legs, everything hanging limp including her expressionless face, she stumbled into paradise's queer playground of dancing adults, popped her eyes at me and threw me a journalistic grenade asking, "They kill subversives don't they?"

Looking into her eyes I saw my rage destiny. Back in bed that night, I took her as a teacher, the Queen of Curiosity, Goddess of Intelligent Reporting, a sacrifice to Mother Rage. I also thanked the bat out of hell.

I didn't have to wait for "divine" voices to intervene anymore. I could find them all around me. The pop star Madonna, that iconoclastic herald of the divine feminine, Religion's "Other Woman," the kind of woman that reasonable clergy love to hate enlightened me in her documentary. As she shared secrets about her life as an artist, mother, and student of Jewish Kabbhala she challenged the notions of god, sex, and power and raised up embodied spirituality as an erotic, ecstatic force. In Israel speaking on behalf of a social cause, Madonna wouldn't claim either Judaism or Israel in her faith. She said she could only speak for herself.

That was when I was reminded; I am an artist, not a saint. I didn't need a greater cause or tradition to claim my relationship with God. Operating on such limited authority isn't rare for artists. A novelist, painter, playwright, or dancer is not an artist if they copy others. As an artist, could I do as Madonna did, speak for myself and let it be enough?

Anxious about the route I was on, I reached out to Ruth. She wrote back,

> *Don't forget how precious you are, and how coura-*
> *geous you are to walk the world with truth paint*
> *smeared all over your entire body! It's a scary time—*
> *don't even try to deny that. In fact, don't deny anything,*
> *especially being in circles where you can be loved....*
> *Affirm to your self that whatever story you have about*
> *any given thing is only a fragment of the reality. It is*
> *profoundly ironic that the good, bad, and ugly has coex-*
> *isted for millions of years. Blow gently on your tight*
> *thoughts and give them a bit more space. You are doing*
> *what you can, and that is good and plenty! Your task:*
> *balance the heat of your truth with cool kindness, espe-*
> *cially towards yourself. Do this every moment you think*
> *about it! Get home safely. More later. Hugging you in the*
> *scary places.*

Even though I didn't know the people on the "Recognition and Standing" committee, I sent them my writing. Would any of them "recognize" me? I researched leave-taking rituals, imagining the plop of fizzy antacid tablets into a cauldron of collective stew, followed by feeding each other dark mouthfuls of devil's food cake. Common sense told me the committee wouldn't go for that. A simple hand washing seemed best. Pontius Pilate washed his hands of the whole Jesus mess. I wasn't washing my hands of Christ, but the parallel didn't escape me.

When the day arrived, Charlotte graciously accompanied me. Ten men and women at a conference table greeted us. I had an hour. A laywoman invited us to place our hands on our hearts and listen. She asked everyone to extend his or her hands to me in a gesture of openness. I saw that they were good people. I knew several were openly gay and lesbian. One man was African-American.

I prepared for questions. Would they tell me why no one had asked me to lead any events, church conferences, or preach in years? Instead, they were genuinely concerned and bewildered and asked me why I wanted to renounce my ordination. I told them that the practices of the Church had become too painful. I could no longer take responsibility for them.

We spent most of the hour discerning who could wash their hands of my ordination. Both the chair of the committee and the regional minister believed ordination was a vow with God into which they couldn't intervene. I challenged, "Would you once again leave me alone in my struggle?" In the end we compromised. As the bowl of water was passed, each committee member chose to wash his or her hands or hold a candle and pray.

I poured water in the basin, prayed aloud my intent, and washed my hands. As the basin passed, half of the committee washed their hands. Half, including the regional minister, lifted the candle, but did not renounce my ordination. Charlotte ended the ritual, praying for us all.

The ritual, like most baptisms, was not cathartic. Yet, it signaled relief. I had dignified my rage. Some in the group were visibly moved.

Had I realized that my protest was about to be quietly buried, that no one at the church that had ordained me would know that I'd renounced my ordination for more than a year, I might have taken further steps. At the time I heard a still, small voice that said, "It's what you do with your own hands that matters most." I'd taken a stand.

A friend sent me words of assurance from Mr. Rogers, the children's TV show icon who said, "The values we care about the deepest, and the movements within society that support those values, command our love. When those things that we care about so deeply become endangered, we become enraged. And what a healthy thing that is! Without it, we would never stand up and speak out for what we believe." I guess I made it to Mr. Roger's neighborhood.

10 | The Choice to Bless the World

Stubborn standers, beware.
planted on twin pillars
of righteousness
and self-righteousness
your footing stiffens
in that precarious pose.
Resist—you stand against.
Consist—you stand with.
Persist—you stand through.
Insist—you stand in.
All stands degrade.
Want peace?
Release your footing.
Dance life's stubborn dance.

PROVIDENCE DICTATED THAT THE FIRST WEEKS after I renounced my ordination, I had three preaching engagements. Could I be trusted to speak to the church? If Love led, then instead of being less qualified, perhaps I was more qualified to preach. InterPlay's body wisdom taught me to navigate by the physicality of grace. I put down my ordination in order to keep choosing things that increase energy, freedom, and spaciousness. Renunciation wasn't just a mere act of anger. Every fiber of my being believed I could do as Rebecca Parker suggested, "Choose to Bless the World."

The choice to bless the world is more than act of will,
A moving forward into the world
With the intention to do good.
It is an act of recognition,
A confession of surprise,
A grateful acknowledgment
That in the midst of a broken world
Unspeakable beauty, grace, and mystery abide.

209

There is an embrace of kindness,
That encompasses all life,
Even yours.
And while there is injustice, anesthetization, or evil
There moves a holy disturbance,
A benevolent rage
A revolutionary love
Protesting, urging, insisting
that which is sacred will not be defiled.
Those who bless the world live their life
As a gesture of thanks
For this beauty
And this rage.
None of us alone can save the world.
Together—that is another possibility waiting.

I entered each church and sang, prayed, improvised, and laughed. I danced where I'd "lost my standing." Come to think of it, aren't those who fall, the first to dance?

Those three churches were another initiation. Afterwards, there were no further preaching engagements. I only learned that I am far from alone. I attracted and joined exiled priests and clergy who had relocated to hermitages, recovery cafes, and remote lakes. In InterPlay I danced with mystics who struggled to find new paradigms for living a healthy earth-friendly, cosmic spirituality in the body politic.

Bit by bit, theological glaciers slid off my back. I opened my wings to the weather. All was not well, but I was well.

Then, Montanez, an InterPlayer and engineering professor at Tennessee State University, astutely asked her logical question, "Cynthia, don't you sing, dance, and pray in InterPlay? Don't you have beliefs? Are you sure InterPlay isn't a religion?"

Perhaps I answered my call, "Hold dance and religion together," too well. Had I gone and made myself another religion, one that dances? I was certainly tempted to be self-righteous, to tell everyone that I had found a better way. This could easily ruin things.

Twenty-five years of chasing the dance of life might have cost me something in my relationship with the church but my faith blossomed. My spiritual practices were mighty. InterPlay was used to unlock the wisdom of the body in work, education, health care, and religion. Hundreds of us witnessed each other adopt an ethic of play and manifest greater joy, beauty, and humor even in the most difficult times. We were changing our world.

As I looked around I began to see many others like me. Experts in various disciplines were keyed into the human capacity to use more of our complexity. Lyall Watson author of *Gifts of Unknown Things* said,

> *Dancing is surely the most basic and relevant of all forms of expression. Nothing else can so effectively give outward form to an inner experience. Poetry and music exist in time. Painting and architecture are a part of space. But only the dance lives at once in both space and time. In it the creator and the thing created, the artist and the expression, are one. Each participant is completely in the other. There could be no better metaphor for an understanding of the cosmos.*
>
> *We begin to realize that our universe is in a sense brought into being by the participation of those involved in it. It is a dance, for participation is its organizing principle. This is the important new concept of quantum mechanics. It takes the place in our understanding of the old notion of observation, of watching without getting involved. Quantum theory says it can't be done. That spectators can sit in their rigid row as long as they like, but there will never be a performance unless at least one of them takes part. And conversely, that it needs only one participant, because that one is the essence of all people and the quintessence of the cosmos.*

Scientific breakthroughs made the news. Brain researchers proved that movement, breath, and spontaneous creativity were efficient ways to stabilize people. Tiny mechanisms called mirror neurons "caught" the moves of others in our bodies, explaining how I can feel it when a child falls and how it is that when a football player runs I sense his motion. Science had uncovered the holy grail of compassion. All we needed to prove was that conscious use of our gluey moves could help us accelerate health and soothe reactionary instincts. Fancy, ancient stuff.

When I saw a newspaper article headlined, "Protestant Reformation Causes Depression" I felt vindicated. Social commentator Barbara Ehrenreich came out with *Dancing in the Streets: A History of Collective Joy* in 2007 after researching the calamitous cultural effects of repressing dance, costume, drum, and public ecstasy. She unmasked the historical forces that outcast dance, sexuality, carnival, and women's power because of their ability to consolidate power and promote rebellion. She cast a particularly harsh light on the church's role in separating dance from moral behavior. She guessed, as I do, that divorcing ourselves from our body, the earth's body, and the bodies of indigenous people contributed to rampant collective melancholy, workaholism, sex addiction, and materialism.

When Ehrenreich came to town, I decorated her book with ribbons and danced over to the San Francisco Commonwealth Club. The wide-eyed scholar behind the podium was admittedly not a dancer. Nothing thrilled me more. She championed something more important, something that belongs to everyone, the dance of life.

In the question and answer period an East Indian man confessed that on trips back to India when he attended public dancing festivities he no longer felt sure that he could dance. He asked Ehrenreich, "How does someone dance again?" Her answer was, "I don't know."

Perhaps the question we need to answer to gain our hearts desire is not "can we dance?" The question is "will we dance?" Forget about steps. Forget about looking good. Let go and dance.

Ehrenreich said that her book was dedicated to her granddaughters. She saw freedom and joy in their dancing. Would they be able to hold onto the gift of life they inherited just by being born? She hoped they would figure this out. But, I worried that elders steeped in western academic training may talk about integration, but if they rarely dance, drum, or practice imaginative technologies their granddaughters would not receive their dancing inheritance. Plodding linear, rational thinking on its own is the least direct route to integration. On the other hand, crazy dancing spirit people arrive at cumulative embodied insight and power in a flash. But, we look odd, like we've lost our minds. Perhaps this is why Spirit consistently gets artists and mystics to lead the way into the future. It's our job to be odd.

The Mayan calendar says that it takes fifty-two cycles around time's spiral to grow up. At age 52 my eyelids drooped over my eyeballs. I'd gained the weight of a middle-aged woman and was sometimes jealous that Mom could retire early from the phone company. Meanwhile, I actively fantasized about donning a Tree of Life costume and parading around with a pack of rainbow serpents. Stranger things have happened.

I didn't have a clue what was to come, but I knew that change was coming fast. The high-wired anxiety of the twenty-first century wasn't working. We were depleting our resources. Stress was constant. Those who could improvise, play, hold hands, dance, find the "Big Body," and stay open to the struggles of those around them were doing best at thriving. In InterPlay we let bodies move, breathe, be with each other, repeating the mantra, "Never underestimate the body's need for reassurance."

I prayed.

> *Hold hands.*
> *Sway.*
> *Breathe.*
> *Sing and cry.*
> *Beat the drum*
> *Beat anything.*
> *Empower spirit,*

Speak,
Let silence be silence
don't let me leave this day
hardly touching those on left or right.

If my first fifty years were training for the years to come, I wanted to be at my best in these increasingly stressful times. How could anyone model ease, creativity, freedom, and joy when even Robert Redford speaking at a graduation ceremony implored the graduates to work for change and to do it quickly? The terrors of global warming, massive economic shifts, overpopulation, and war were upon us.

I started seeing the number 11 pop up everywhere. 11:11 a.m. 1:11 p.m. 9/11, 7/11, 1/11. It was eerie. I toyed with crackpot theories. Was it a result of the digital age? Clocks show specific numbers. I googled the question, "What about all these elevens?" and got the website of psychic Uri Geller. Apparently other people reported repeatedly seeing the number eleven, too.

Numerologists see 11 as a number of dramatic movement. As I studied it I realized it was two ones standing side-by-side like a gateway. I thought of my side-by-side collaboration with Phil and so many of my dancing companions. One plus one plus one plus one. When each one joins hands, moving together nothing can stop us. We dance.

It could be that the number eleven was a reflection of the parallel permanent creases in most foreheads, the modern sign of our inner beasts. I joined meetings for the "serenity challenged" and finally put rage on my "don't share with others" list. I began reciting a daily prayer penned by nineteenth century Protestant theologian, Reinhold Niebuhr. He too must have struggled to find peace in the academy and church. "God grant me the serenity, to accept the things I cannot change, the courage to change the things I can, and the wisdom to know the difference." Day by day serenity grew.

The more serenity I felt the more I realized that it resembled neutrality. I meditated on the vast unconditional neutral regard basic to the Universe. Its ecstasy is rooted in the simplest of all freedoms: to dance the dance of life without getting too overly entangled in it all. Mystics who encountered the cosmic dance before me had painted hundreds of visual and word pictures to show the way back to the dance. In the 1900's C.S Lewis wrote in *Perelandra*.

> *In the plan of the Great Dance plans without number interlock, and each movement becomes in its season the breaking into flower of the whole design to which all else had been directed. Thus each is equally at the centre and none are there by being equals, but some by giving place and some by receiving it, the small things by their smallness and the great by their greatness, and all the patterns linked and looped together by the unions of a people kneeling with a sceptred love.*

The Dance of Life and the Tree of Life were always at ease. They always had enough. They welcomed every part, every being, without suspect.

Hundreds of InterPlayers formed a leader's circle. We went to Malawi, India, Bali, New Zealand, Australia, Morocco, Germany, and Brazil. We applied our wisdom in families, professions, non-profits and international relationships. Every place we danced and sang became a holy place. We invited more and more people to tell their stories. The dance of life was sneaky deep. We were healing. Some would have called these days the worst days in the history of the world. But we were running light-footed toward the center of our cities.

To keep up I had to let go and hold on at the same time. I let go of ordination, my teaching job at Pacific School of Religion, my work on the local UN board, and my role in Wing It! When I wanted to lie down in a heap, give up, or retreat, somebody would invite me to do a hand dance, sing my song, or join in the general dance. Stepping back into the dance of life made me sane, gave me hope, and showed the way.

I found myself singing a song that I sang in one of my first music-dance and drama liturgies from the 1980's. It was based on a prophetic biblical poem.

> *The old shall dream new dreams*
> *The young shall see a mighty vision*
> *On the day that love has made*
> *We will end our hateful division*
> *Joy shall come to the city streets*
> *When our hearts with life together beat.*
> *The rich ones poor ones shall bow down*
> *To the children who shall lead us.*
> *Oh people come and sing your song*
> *Sing this song together*
> *Joy shall come to this strange land*
> *When we love each other.*
> *When we love each other.*

I still believed these words. But, voices, visions, none of these were necessary anymore. I had all the information I needed. I just hoped that the Universe could give me the stamina to live what I know. No doubt, it would. For young or old, the universe loves a dancer.

Appendices

Cynthia's 13 "Deals"

1. *Religious exclusion:* Jesus the Lord language implies that Jewish and other faiths are "less than." I no longer tolerate "THE" Christ, Savior, Victor, King, or Conqueror names that diminish any other views of God.

2. *Evangelism:* I can no longer support a religion whose primary dictate is to convert others. Violence, greed, and disrespect for other cultures results. George Bush's crusade is another example.

3. *Racial apathy:* Without conscious processes for telling truth about our racial patterning, we lack instinctive outrage at racial injustice. I want to be in communities that are ready to do the emotional work of healing racism.

4. *Word idolatry:* Words limit us to one voice at a time, decrease the chorus of diversity, cover over emotion and dull down listeners. I seek more embodied, diverse, direct experiences of Spirit.

5. *Solo preachers:* A single leader, whether woman or man, emphasizes the wisdom of ONE. Listeners tend to mistrust their own wisdom. Talented people should lead, but not from center stage. I want to hear many people struggling, failing, and finding hope.

6. *Wound-based boundaries:* Ministry institutionalizes shepherds who oversee a flock. Mutuality is prevented in this paradigm. Desire for adult spiritual friendship is not a church construct.

7. *Repressing the Feminine:* Male Christian imagery pervades hymnody, prayer, theology, architecture, and artistic construction. To become more compassionate, feminine ways are essential for balance. I want a thousand God-She's for every God-He.

8. *Reason over imagination:* Rationality plays emperor over complex realities. Things that can't be described in ideas require symbolic communication. Imagination is an essential form of intelligence for complex communications.

9. *Suspicion of mysticism:* Intellectual suspicion predominates Christianity. The methods of Jesus' embodied soul craft and the skills that naturally abide in the arts can restore connection with God.

10. *Repressed sexuality:* Excluding erotic energy in church requires the church to push "boundaries." No touch, no health. I want people to learn to play safely in their bodies.

11. *Dismissing the body:* The refusal to embrace physicality as the locus of blessing is heretical to Jesus' teaching. Lip service to incarnation is not enough. I want to deepen the collective wisdom in our bodies.

12. *Suppressed laughter and tears:* Church piety suppresses spiritual honesty and direct experience as we disallow our bodies to be moved. I want to laugh and cry in community.

13. *Over-scripted worship:* Scripts focus on controlling experience rather than on bigger spirit and truth. Open improvisational structures that invite mystery allow present time spiritual conversation in God's presence.

Thirteen Body Wisdoms

1. *InterPlay is social glue.* It bonds people faster than the speed of the mind. Easygoing dance, play, and storytelling are like high speed Internet. Too much talk is like using dialup.

2. *InterPlay connects diverse people faster.* When the body is our common ground, movers more quickly share the content of life, the pull of gravity, energy, touch, emotion, sense, and limitations.

3. *InterPlay dramatically increases ease and relaxation in groups and leaders.* It is a natural serotonin-reuptake inhibitor.

4. *InterPlay activates creativity.* When the whole body gets going, our nerves fire, serotonin leaps, cortisol stabilizes, and ideas pop. InterPlay unbottles ideas, memories, and soul-utions. You don't have to wait to be creative. It's part of the path!

5. *InterPlay activates our higher power.* In a collective body that integrates action and thought, higher power is no longer mere thought, but felt in the dialogue of forms interacting with the universe of imagination. Some people call this God, although naming it is not necessary to receive the benefits.

6. *InterPlay generates social welfare.* When each person moves in ways congruent with who they are and how they feel in community, we better honor and respond to each person's need for healing, service, and expression.

7. *InterPlay creates sanity.* Realigning mind, body, heart, and spirit by engaging whole systems, in a matter of minutes, groups of people restore themselves to easy-going sanity.

8. *InterPlay rehumanizes, restoring and healing us from community wear and tear.* On a Friday morning at my studio ten of us warm up in an easy sequence that does not ask that you know your right foot from your left. We swing our arms, thrust out our energy in short spurts for a few seconds, and then glide into an extended time that begins with Fake Tai Chi. There is permission to do absolutely nothing but be still. Many people wind up lying on the floor, revealing that most of us are tired even at 10:00 in the morning. After ten or fifteen minutes these adults naturally choose to interplay. Their elbows touch and their feet spontaneously connect in a circle where we gather news, highlights, and things that are too heavy for us to carry alone. Ending in improvised movement and song we bless the collective. People look relaxed and surprised that they like each other.

9. *InterPlay fosters contentment.* Neither expensive, time consuming, or ultra-disciplined, InterPlay uplifts everyday content. People learn that they don't have to produce to be content. It's a very uncapitalistic serum for peace.

10. *InterPlay normalizes body image issues.* People learn to engage with one another's dystrophies, birthmarks, burns, scars, pudge, and mental idiosyncrasies, welcoming each body as a part of the dance of life.

11. *InterPlay is a freedom contagion.* It democratizes. Harnessing the revolutionary energies similar to Woodstock, anti-apartheid South Africa, and the dance of children, InterPlay reclaims the power of "original innocence," through adult, and intergenerational forms. Everyone gets to contribute.

Resources

New Revised Standard Bible. Iowa Falls, IA: World Bible Publishers, 1997.

The Tree of Life. New York: Society for the Study of Myth and Tradition, 1989.

Adams, Doug. *Congregational Dancing in Christian Worship*. Austin, TX: The Sharing Company, 1980.

Agar, Michael. *Language Shock: Understanding the Culture of Conversation*. New York: William Morrow, 1994.

Berryman, Jeff. *Leaving Ruin: A Novel*. Orange, CA: New Leaf Books, 2002.

Boal, Augusto. *Theatre of the Oppressed*. New York: Theatre Communications Group, 1985.

Cameron, Anne. *Daughters of Copper Woman*. Vancouver, BC: Press Gang Publishers, 1981.

Csikszentmihalyi, Mihaly. *Flow: The Psychology of Optimal Experience*. New York: Harper & Row, 1990.

DeSola, Carla. *The Spirit Moves: A Handbook of Dance and Prayer*. Washington: Liturgical Conference, 1977.

Ehrenreich, Barbara. *Dancing in the Streets: A History of Collective Joy.* New York: Metropolitan Books, 2007.

Elliott, J. K. *The Apocryphal New Testament: A Collection of Apocryphal Christian Literature in an English Translation.* Oxford: Clarendon Press, 1993.

Finnerty, Adam Daniel. *No More Plastic Jesus: Global Justice and Christian Lifestyle.* New York: Dutton, 1977.

Freire, Paulo. *Pedagogy of the Oppressed.* New York: Continuum, 2003.

Goleman, Daniel. *Social Intelligence: The New Science of Human Relationships.* New York: Bantam Books, 2006.

Hammerschlag, Carl A. *The Dancing Healers: A Doctor's Journey of Healing with Native Americans.* San Francisco: Harper & Row, 1989.

Hooks, Bell. *Salvation: Black People and Love.* New York: Perennial, 2001.

Ingerman, Sandra. *Soul Retrieval: Mending the Fragmented Self.* San Francisco: HarperSanFrancisco, 1991.

Jones, Laurie Beth. *The Path: Creating Your Mission Statement for Work and for Life.* New York: Hyperion, 1996.

Kaestli, Jean-Daniel. "Response [to Dewey, Arthur. 'The Hymn in the Acts of John: Dance as Hermeneutic.' Semeia 38 (1986) 67-80.]." Semeia 38 (1986): 81-88.

Karasek, David. *Images of the Spirit.* Omega Liturgical Dance Company, 1976.

King, Ruth. *Healing Rage: Women Making Inner Peace Possible.* Berkeley, CA: Sacred Spaces Press, 2004.

Langer, Susanne Katherina Knauth. *Feeling and Form: A Theory of Art Developed from Philosophy in a New Key.* New York: Scribner, 1953.

MacDonald, Sarah. *Holy Cow: An Indian Adventure.* New York: Broadway Books, 2002.

Marechal, Paul. *Dancing Madly Backwards: A Journey into God.* New York: Crossroad, 1982.

McBride, James. *The Color of Water: A Black Man's Tribute to His White Mother*. New York: Riverhead Books, 1996.

Owens, Virginia Stem. *And the Trees Clap Their Hands: Faith, Perception, and the New Physics*. Grand Rapids, MI: W.B. Eerdmans, 1983.

Paul Winter Consort. "Lay Down Your Burdens." Common Ground. A&M, 1978.

Pham, Andrew X. *Catfish and Mandala: A Two-Wheeled Voyage through the Landscape and Memory of Vietnam*. New York: Picador, 2000.

Porter, Phil. *The Slightly Mad Rantings of a Body Intellectual Part One*. Oakland, CA: Wing It! Press, 2005.

Rock, Judith, and Norman Mealy. *Performer as Priest and Prophet: Restoring the Intuitive in Worship through Music and Dance*. San Francisco: Harper & Row, 1988.

Schnarch, David Morris. *Passionate Marriage: Love, Sex, and Intimacy in Emotionally Committed Relationships*. New York: Holt, 1997.

Somé, Malidoma Patrice. *The Healing Wisdom of Africa: Finding Life Purpose through Nature, Ritual, and Community*. New York: Tarcher/Putnam, 1999.

St. Denis, Ruth. *An Unfinished Life: An Autobiography*. New York: Harper, 1939.

Taylor, Barbara Brown. *Leaving Church: A Memoir of Faith*. San Francisco: HarperSanFrancisco, 2006.

Taylor, Margaret Fisk. *The Art of the Rhythmic Choir: Worship through Symbolic Movement*. New York: Harper, 1950.

Thompson, Robert Farris. *African Art in Motion: Icon and Act*. Los Angeles: University of California Press, 1979.

Thurman, Howard. *The Luminous Darkness: A Personal Interpretation of the Anatomy of Segregation and the Ground of Hope*. Richmond, IN: Friends United Press, 1965.

Udall, Brady. *The Miracle Life of Edgar Mint: A Novel*. New York: Vintage Contemporaries, 2001.

Watts, Trish. *Deep Waters*. Willow Music, 1994.

Weiss, Brian L. *Many Lives, Many Masters: The True Story of a Prominent Psychiatrist, His Young Patient, and the Past-Life Therapy that Changed Both of Their Lives*. New York: Simon & Schuster, 1988.

Whitelaw, Ginny, and Betsy Wetzig. *Move to Greatness: Focusing the Four Essential Energies of a Whole and Balanced Leader*. Boston: Nicholas Brealey International, 2008.

Whitman, Walt. *Leaves of Grass*. Garden City, NY: Doubleday, Page, & Co., 1926.

Wuellner, Flora Slosson. *Prayer, Stress, and Our Inner Wounds*. Nashville, TN: Upper Room, 1985.

Zdenek, Marilee, and Marge Belcher Champion. *God Is a Verb!* Waco, TX: Word Books, 1974.

Printed in the United States
135632LV00001B/10/P